The Complete Guide to
the Best Pubs in
Dublin

Kevin Martin

ORPEN PRESS

Published by
Orpen Press
Upper Floor, Unit K9
Greenogue Business Park
Rathcoole
Co. Dublin
Ireland

email: info@orpenpress.com
www.orpenpress.com

ISBN 978-1-78605-070-0

Printed in Dublin by SPRINTprint Ltd

This book is dedicated to my wife, Maria, with whom I spent some great times in the pubs of Dublin.

Acknowledgements

I would like to thank the following people for their help: Ann Ambrose, Rosita Boland, Tom Butler, Maria Carroll, Olivia Carroll, Ciara Canavan, Eamon Casey, Phelim Conway, Phionna Convey, Ann Convey, Bernie Ryan Costello, Howard Dee Crean, Fionnuala Feeny, Carol Ferson, Donna Ferson, Ashling Flynn, Fidelma Gallagher, Carine Geluck, John Geraghty, Kevin Groden, Mary Groden, Richard Johnson, Kieran O'Hora, David Lydon, Olivia Needham, Kevin Mallon, Sharon Marley, David Martin, Raymond Martin, DArcy MacKay, Ronan McCool, Una Morris, Patricia McLoughlin, Michael McVann, Patricia McVann, Richard Moyles, Aileen Mulhern, Damian Mulkearns, John Mulkearns, Mary O'Donnell, Kevin O'Donoghue, Neil Paul, Kathy Quinn, Tara Reece, Marc Roberts, Tim Rogers, Marguerite Rowland, Aideen Ryan, Áine Ryan, Majella Sharkey, John Sharkey, Breege Timoney, members of the Old Dublin Pub Group on Facebook, and all the other people who made suggestions and comments.

I would particularly like to thank Eileen O'Brien and all at Orpen Press.

THE COMPLETE GUIDE TO THE BEST PUBS IN DUBLIN

Kevin Martin

Contents

Preface xiii

1. A Short History of the Irish Pub 1
Introduction.. 1
The First Pubs in Ireland (kind of) 1
The Role of Religious Orders 3
The Normans 5
Ale Brewing.. 6
The First Pub Laws 7
The Glorious Victorian Era 9
The Literary Pubs of Dublin 9
Changing Times 10
A Note on Licensing Laws.. *11*

2. Dublin City Centre South 12
1. The Bailey.. 12
    The First Bloomsday *15*
2. The Bank Bar and Restaurant................................ 16
3. The Bar With No Name... 18
    The 'Holy Hour' *19*
4. The Bernard Shaw 19
5. The Bleeding Horse.. 21
    A Dublin Pub in the Nineteenth Century *24*
6. Bowe's 25
    Easter Rising 1916 and Dublin Pubs.................... *27*
7. The Brazen Head 28
8. Bruxelles... 31
    What Not to Order in a Dublin Pub: The 'Irish Car Bomb'...... *34*
9. Cafe en Seine 34

10. Cassidy's 36
    US Presidents and Irish Pubs 38
11. Davy Byrne's 39
12. Devitt's 43
    Family Names and Irish Pubs 44
13. Doheny and Nesbitt 45
    The Victorian Pub... 48
14. The Duke 49
    Snugs... 51
15. Farrier and Draper... 52
16. The Ferryman 53
    One that Got Away: The Irish House Pub 55
17. The George 56
18. The Gravity Bar at the Guinness Storehouse 58
19. Grogan's/Castle Lounge.................................... 59
    The Lounge Bar Revolution................................ 62
20. Hartigan's 63
21. The Horseshoe Bar in the Shelbourne Hotel 64
    Irish Coffee 67
22. The International Bar 67
23. Jimmy Rabbitte's 70
24. John Fallon's (The Capstan Bar) 71
    Dublin's Smallest Pub: The Dawson Lounge 74
25. Kehoe's 74
    James Joyce and Dublin Pubs 76
26. The Library Bar at the Central Hotel 78
27. The Long Hall 79
28. The Lord Edward 82
29. Mary's Bar 84
    Spirit Grocer... 86
30. McDaid's 87
31. Mulligan's.. 90
    Strange Things in Dublin Pubs............................ 93
32. Neary's 93
33. The Norseman 95
    Temple Bar 96
34. O'Connell's Bar... 97

35. O'Donoghue's 98
36. The Old Stand 100
    Saint Patrick's Day and Pubs *102*
37. O'Neill's 103
    The Pubs in James Joyce's Dubliners *104*
38. The Palace Bar 105
39. Peruke and Periwig 108
40. P. Mac's 109
41. The Porterhouse Central 110
    The Craft Beer Revolution *111*
42. The Porterhouse, Temple Bar 112
43. Ruin Bar 113
44. Searson's 113
45. The Stag's Head 115
46. The Swan 117
    The Twelve Pubs of Christmas *119*
47. Toner's 121
48. The Vintage Cocktail Club 123
49. Whelan's 126

3. Dublin City Centre North **128**
1. The Church 128
   Guinness *130*
2. The Confession Box 131
   The Irish War of Independence *134*
3. The Hacienda 135
   Matt Talbot and the 'Demon Drink' *136*
4. Jack Nealon's 137
   Kips *138*
5. Madigan's 139
   Smoking Ban *141*
6. The Oval 141
7. Pantibar 143
   'Pantigate' *144*
8. The Piper's Corner 145
   The Long Story of Good Friday *146*
9. Ryan's of Parkgate Street 147
   When the Pubs Saved the Economy *149*

10. Slattery's of Capel Street 150
    Early Houses *151*

4. Dublin City South Suburbs................................... 152
1. The Dropping Well 152
    Bona Fide Pubs.. *153*
2. The Oarsman 154
    'Gastropubs' *155*
3. The Old Spot... 155
4. Royal Oak, Kilmainham 156
5. Slattery's of Rathmines................................... 157
    The Day Formerly Known as Arthur's Day *159*
6. The Yellow House 160

5. Dublin City North Suburbs 162
1. The Barber's.. 162
    Licensed Vintners' Association *163*
2. The Cobblestone 164
    Music Sessions in Irish Pubs *165*
3. Fagan's 166
4. Gaffney's of Fairview 168
    The Rounds System... *169*
5. The Gravediggers/Kavanagh's.......................... 170
    Publicans as Undertakers *173*
6. Harry Byrne's 174
7. The Hole in the Wall 175
8. The Hut/Mohan's 177
    Shebeens *179*
9. L Mulligan Grocer... 179
10. Walsh's 181

6. Dublin South County...................................... 183
1. The Blue Light 183
2. Finnegan's 184
    A Fourteen-Year-Long Pub Strike........................ *185*
3. Johnnie Fox's.. 186

7. Dublin North County...................................... 188
1. Gibney's 188

2. The Harbour Bar (formerly the Cock Tavern) 189
   Irish Civil War *190*
3. The Man O'War Bar and Restaurant 191
4. Stoop Your Head 192

8. West Dublin **194**
1. Strawberry Hall 194
   Pub Numbers *196*

Index **197**

Preface

The public house - or pub - has long been a central component of the social and cultural life of the city of Dublin and
in the wider Irish countryside. This book is not a personal
list but rather a guide to those pubs most loved by those who
know them best. It is based on extensive surveys, question-
naires and interviews. It also factors in the myriad similar lists
compiled by others. A cursory search of cyberspace indicates
an incredible number of pub guides to Dublin, a sure indication of the institution's enduring popularity. There is no other
city on earth with such a plethora of fine drinking houses.
Such are the number of great pubs in Dublin it would have
been easy to include 200 in this guide and still have some in
reserve. Indeed, in the course of research almost 300 pubs
were mentioned. Some will see glaring omissions while others
will contest the inclusion of some establishments, such is the
debate engendered by the topic of favourite pubs. Despite the
frenetic evolution of society over the last number of decades
the Dublin pub has managed to survive and, after a recent
rough spell, thrive once again. Let this guide serve as an introduction to the topic. While it includes those pubs that are held
in highest esteem and have the highest profiles there are many
other hidden gems that will equally enthral the visitor. Should
anyone consider any omission criminal please do not hesitate
to contact me at kevinmartin421@gmail.com.

A Short History of the Irish Pub

Leopold Bloom, the central character in James Joyce's fictional masterpiece *Ulysses*, famously said it would be a good puzzle to walk across Dublin without passing a pub. The problem was only solved in 2011 by software developer Rory McCann using a computer program; even then McCann could not find a route without passing a hotel, while he also had to rule out restaurants with licences to serve alcohol. McCann's route runs from Blackhorse Avenue to Baggot Street, going through Stoneybatter, past Saint James's Gate (the home of Guinness) down Bride Street, across York Street, past Saint Stephen's Green, detouring through the Iveagh Gardens, and down Adelaide Road. McCann modified the route in 2014 to avoid passing any hotels and, fittingly, it now goes over the new James Joyce Bridge. It is a testament to the centrality of the pub in Irish culture and society – particularly in Dublin – that this conundrum took 110 years to solve.

The First Pubs in Ireland (kind of)

The word 'pub' – short for public house – is used to describe a premises licensed to sell alcohol to all those who are allowed, by law, to purchase it therein. The term 'public house' was first used to differentiate such an establishment from a private members' club. It is a simple concept understood across the world. In Ireland the pub has long been the central component of social culture, a home from home for so many people. Why has the pub evolved to be such a central part of Irish society? Why is it that you see Irish pubs in

Lima, or Honolulu, or Ulaanbaatar, and not Estonian pubs? What factors have underpinned the development of the Irish pub?

One thing is certain: the central role of the pub in Ireland did not just happen by chance. Above all else it is the deeply embedded tradition of hospitality in Irish culture which has resulted in pubs being such a significant component of the built and social landscape. Hospitality, conviviality and generosity have always been central to Irish society. In ancient Ireland a man was reckoned rich not by what he owned but by what he gave, and the right hand of the generous man was said to be longer than the left. Irish Brehon Law – first codified in the fifth century to regulate the then feudal country – stipulated that each local king or queen was required to have his or her own version of a pub to treat all those who prevailed upon their hospitality. The *bruidean* (usually translated as hostel), as this establishment was called, had to be run by an accomplished *bruigu* (sometimes translated as brewer but closer in meaning to hospitaller) and operated according to a code of strictly enforced rules. The bruigu had to provide 'a never dry cauldron, a dwelling on a public road and a welcome to every face'. He had to provide hospitality to all those who requested it in his hostel. It was nothing like a hostel as we now understand the term but more like a super gastropub with free accommodation, entertainment, food and drink. If the local king or queen was adjudged to have fallen short of the required standards the result was harsh. Breas, one of the ancient kings of Ireland, lost his title because of his lack of hospitality: 'Breas did not grease their knives. In vain they came to visit Breas. Their breath did not smell of ale at the banquet.'

The rules pertaining to the *bruidean* were non-negotiable. It had to be located at a crossroads; have four doors, one on each of the approaching routes; have torch-bearing greeters on a lawn outside the building so nobody would pass by unwelcomed; and stay open 24 hours a day. There were also strict rules on the provision of food. The *bruigu* was required to have three uncooked red meats butchered and ready to cook, three stewed meats cooked and kept heated, and three types of live animals ready to slaughter at short notice. He was also required to keep three sacks of provisions at hand at all times. The first had to contain malt for brewing ale, the second wheat to make bread, and the third salt to enhance the flavour of the food. Additionally, three different cheering sounds had to be heard in the hostel all the time: those of ale makers going happily about their work, those of servers bringing alcohol from the cauldron, and those of young men playing chess. If the brewer fulfilled and maintained these conditions his job attracted a number of perks. He was allowed to have as many servants as the king, was given a tract of land to grow the raw materials for brewing, and was allowed to hold a magistrate's licence. He was also in charge of resolving land disputes, and hosting political meetings and elections. He was even allowed to sit beside the king at any feast or celebration, and was entitled to the next best cut of meat after His Majesty. Only harpists, poets and storytellers could rise above their birth station in the same way as the king's publican.

The respect given to the masters of music and the spoken word is also instructive in further understanding the emergence of public house culture in Ireland. Despite Ireland's deserved reputation as a cradle of many internationally renowned writers, the written word came late to the country. Ireland was primarily an oral or 'bardic' culture (from the word 'bard', a professional poet in old Celtic cultures) and those who could master the spoken word in verse and story were highly esteemed. Skilled storytellers were revered and the most talented poets travelled the country writing poems in praise of nobility for generous fees. The combination of the legal requirements for hospitality and the regard with which masters of the spoken word were held established a legacy of the atmosphere which defines the essence of the Irish pub: both hospitality and communal oral communication were privileged from the earliest days of Irish society – and remain the defining characteristics of a good pub to this day.

The Role of Religious Orders

However, the brewer's hostel was not the only free bar in early Ireland. Many Irish monks were skilled brewers who had originally brought their skills back from trips to the fertile crescent of Mesopotamia – modern-day Turkey, Iraq and Iran. They too provided alcohol with food to passing travellers while keeping their own thirsts satisfied. Cistercian monks at Jerpoint Abbey in County Kilkenny, for example, were allowed drink a gallon of ale per day. Saint Columbanus, a sixth-century Irish missionary priest and skilled brewer, had an interesting last wish: 'to die in the brew house with ale placed in my mouth when I am expiring.' Unfortunately this did not eventuate – he died of a heart attack on a pilgrimage to Rome – but he did have the useful ability to transform water into beer, and once reputedly turned enough water into beer to satisfy 60 thirsty pilgrims at a monastery in Fontaines, France. Columbanus could reverse the process too. According to his biographer Jonas, he turned a cauldron of beer into water by blowing on it at a pagan festival in Bobbio, Italy, after taking exception to a group worshipping a pagan god.

Saint Brigit, one of the most revered of Irish saints, was also a gifted ale brewer and once came to the assistance of a thirsty party of lepers. When the lepers came looking for beer her supplies were exhausted but she noticed water being prepared for baths nearby. She blessed it and 'transformed it into the best beer which she drew copiously for the thirsty'. 'Saint Brigit's Ale Feast', an eleventh-century poem attributed to her, describes a true beer lover:

I'd like to give a lake of beer to God.
I'd love the heavenly
Host to be tippling there
For all eternity.
I'd love the men of Heaven to live with me,
To dance and sing.

If they wanted, I'd put at their disposal
Vats of suffering
I'd sit with the men, the women and God
There by the lake of beer.
We'd be drinking good health forever
And every drop would be a prayer.

Saint Patrick, patron saint of Ireland, reputedly had his own brewer and personal confessor called Meascan. Patrick's preferred brew is said to have been very sweet with hints of bog myrtle and heather, and with a low alcohol content. Monks were often expert herbalists and Meascan was particularly known for the addition of gentian to his ale. As a further indication of the role of the religious in Ireland's drinking history it is instructive to note that the tradition of brewing in Thomas Street in Dublin - now home to the world-famous Guinness brewing facility - began with the monks of Saint Thomas' Abbey in the thirteenth century.

The Normans

The history of Ireland is littered with invasions, not generally of benefit to the natives. At least the Normans (or Anglo-Normans as they are sometimes called) brought their taverns and the designation of 'vintner' to traders in alcohol. The word 'tavern' - originally from the Latin *taberna*, meaning hut - was first used in Ireland when the Norman French occupied parts of Ireland in the twelfth century. The Normans were wine lovers and imported the best from their homeland. At first this alcohol was managed by wine merchants - known as 'vintners' from the French word *vin* for wine - and delivered to the cellars of the castles of the Norman lords who largely resided inside the Pale, an area surrounding greater Dublin under their control. (The term 'outside the pale' came to describe the rest of Ireland. Thus, the Normans brought more than just alcohol-related words to the country). 'Vintner' later became a word commonly used to describe purveyors of all alcohol and the Licensed Vintners' Association (LVA) is the name of the organisation representing the interests of publicans in Dublin city and county and Bray, Co. Wicklow to this day. (If you want to really impress your friends about your knowledge of Irish pub culture you can mention that the publicans in Ireland who live 'outside the Pale' are represented by the Vintners' Federation of Ireland (VFI).)

Occasionally the Norman wine dealers held tasting events when new stock was imported and, over time, they began to sell the surplus at the point of storage. These taverns became meeting places where alcohol and food were served and issues of the day discussed. Dublin's Winetavern Street, referred to as *vicus tabernariorum vini* (the street of the wine taverner) in Latin, was the main centre of distribution and retail. In 1979 archaeologists found pewter 'tavern tokens' dumped in a refuse pit during a nearby excavation. These were used to buy alcohol when currency was in short supply but became obsolete when the round farthing was introduced by Edward I in 1271. Some of them are on display in the National Museum on Kildare Street.

Ale Brewing

While the Normans and the elite consumed their wines, ale was largely the drink of the lower classes; it was much cheaper to produce and usually sold separately in alehouses. These premises were often nothing more than a simple room attached to the residence of the manufacturer. Ale was overwhelmingly produced by women, referred to as 'alewives'. Many were actually widows, but it was also a common occupation for unmarried and young women. The profit margin was slight after oats and barley were paid for. When fresh ale was ready the alewife raised a stick or a flag over her door – sometimes referred to as an 'ale wand' – to alert potential customers. It was important to sell the ale immediately as it spoiled quickly. The local ale brewer's home became the 'local' meeting house, or simply 'the local', a word used nowadays to distinguish a pub in which a customer most frequently drinks.

Alewives and alehouses were not always popular with the authorities and were the subject of frequent legislator initiatives. In 1455, for example, female ale brewers were warned by decree not to adulterate the brewing process by adding straw. If a woman was found guilty of selling substandard ale she was fined and if she reoffended her operation could be closed down and she could be flogged. 'The Alewives' Invitation to Married Men and Bachelors', a popular nineteenth-century ballad, may provide a clue as to the nature of some of the shenanigans – another Irish word – which might have occurred in alehouses:

Therefore take my Counsel, & Alewives don't trust,
For when you have wasted, and spent all you have,

Then out of Doors she will you headlong thrust
Calling you Rascal, and shirking Knave.
But so long as you have Money, come early or late,
You shall have her at Command, or else her Maid Kate.

British soldier and writer Barnaby Rich was particularly unimpressed
by the alehouses when he visited Dublin in 1561 to provide a report
for Queen Elizabeth I: 'There is no merchandise so vendable. It is
the very marrow of the common wealth in Dublin. The whole profit
of the towne stands upon alehouses and the selling of ale. There
are whole streets of taverns and it is a rare thing to find a street in
Dublin without a tavern, as it is to find a tavern without a strumpet.'
In *A New Description of Ireland* Rich made it abundantly clear that
he was a fan of neither the Irish nor alcohol. Sundays were particularly troublesome, he wrote, because 'every filthy alehouse' was full
of people 'drunkening and quaffing and sometimes defiling themselves with more abominable practices'.

The First Pub Laws

Arguably the defining responses to the laws pertaining to pubs in
Ireland for the first 300 years were ignorance and subterfuge. In
essence much of the legislation of the British colonial authorities
was completely ignored. In 1613 the Register of Patents and Inven-
tions recorded the first Elizabethan licences issued for Irish taverns.
Seven licences were issued that year, while only one was granted
in 1614. In 1616 a further seven licences were allowed. In reality
there was little control and illegal outlets, called shebeens (yet
another word the Irish have given to the English language), were
rampant. Indeed, few places were safe from the trade in alcohol. In
1633, Thomas Stafford, Earl of Wentworth and the Lord Deputy of
Ireland, complained to Archbishop Laud of London about the use of
the crypt in Christ Church Cathedral – the most important religious
establishment in Dublin at that time – as a place of sale for alcohol
and tobacco.

The first law against the establishment of new unlicensed
premises was enacted in 1635, and it was damning of those already

in existence: 'Many mischiefes and inconveniences doe arise from the excessive number of alehouses, from the erection of them in woods, bogges, and other unfit places, many of them not in towneships, but dispersedly in dangerous places and kept by unknown persons not under-taken for, whereby many times they have become receptacles for rebels and other malefactors and harbours of gamesters and other idle, disordered and unprofitable livers, and that those who keep those alehouses for the most part are not fitted or furnished to lodge or entertaine travelers in any decent manner.'

If an individual wanted to establish a public house from then on he would have to provide 'two beds for strangers' and 'sell provisions to travellers at reasonable prices'. There should be no drunkenness, gambling or 'unlawful games' and it would be illegal to 'harbour improper persons'. The Act, like those that went before, was spectacularly unsuccessful.

In 1685 the Lord's Day Act allowed policemen to enter pubs for the first time and from then on licences were supposed to be renewed annually. This legislation also prohibited Sunday trading during the hours of worship and made it illegal to marry in a pub.

The development of stage coach travel, mail coach lines and a national postal service during the nineteenth century advanced the pub trade. Coaching inns with alcohol, food and lodgings became more common. The mid-nineteenth century saw the development of the rail network, allowing greater movement of goods and people, and led to a further expansion of the licensed trade. Many of these inns were rudimentary and did not always meet with visitors' expectations. Englishman Edward Wakefield travelled through Ireland in 1810, staying in a few, and recorded his opinions in *An Account of Ireland, Statistical and Political*. The buildings, he wrote, were inferior to those found in England and the innkeepers were unwelcoming and rude: 'In an Irish inn, the eye ... is everywhere disgusted with filthy objects. The olfactory nerves are also affected by the noxious effluvia arising from the same cause.' If there was a waiter present he was likely to be so ridiculous in appearance he would form an excellent subject for 'eminent caricaturists'.

The Glorious Victorian Era

The late nineteenth century and early twentieth century was the first golden age of the Dublin pub. Queen Victoria reigned over the kingdom of Great Britain and Ireland between 1876 and 1901 at a time of huge industrial change. While Ireland did not benefit in the same way economically as the British mainland, the construction of a new wave of public houses was indicative of the higher standards expected by the more eminent Victorians and the newfound respectability of the role of the publican. The sixteen remaining fully Victorian pubs – as well as many others with Victorian features – are a central component of the built heritage of Dublin.*

The Literary Pubs of Dublin

These days so many pubs in Dublin claim a literary link that it can be sometimes hard to separate fact from fiction, but there is no doubt that there is a huge overlap between the hostelries of the city and the creative output of the literati of the past. In *An Age of Innocence: Irish Culture 1930-1960*, Brian Fallon points out that even though the literary pubs of Dublin only had a lifespan of roughly forty years 'they are interwoven into the cultural, intellectual and social life of the period as Vienna's coffee houses are with its golden age, or the classic cafes and bars of Paris are with its great period from the years just before the First World War to the decade after the second.'

The Catholic Church and state did not look entirely favourably on the literary and artistic communities of post-independent Ireland. It was a virtually theocratic society and among the ranks of the literati the state saw subversive elements whom they wished to quieten. The public house was one place where these men – they were virtually all men – could freely express their opinions with likeminded souls.

---

* The sixteen remaining Dublin Victorian pubs are: the Palace; Toner's; Doheny & Nesbitt's; the Swan; the Long Hall; Slattery's of Capel Street; the Stag's Head; Ryan's of Parkgate Street; the International; Gaffney's of Fairview; The Hut, Phibsboro; Bowe's; Kehoe's; Sorrento Lounge/Finnegan's, Dalkey; Cassidy's of Camden Street; and the Norseman, Temple Bar.

It may have been a poor substitute for wider critical acclaim and financial reward, but in a repressive regime many, such as Patrick Kavanagh, Brendan Behan and Flann O'Brien, found solace in the sublimation of alcohol and conversation in those pubs where they were welcomed.

Changing Times

The latter part of the twentieth century witnessed huge changes in pubs in Ireland, and Dublin in particular. From the 1960s Irish society began a gradual transition. Feminism, increased prosperity and the loosening of the stranglehold of the Catholic Church changed socialising patterns. Women became part of a more vibrant pub scene and lounge bars were constructed throughout the country. The 1960s also witnessed a boom in traditional and folk music sessions in pubs, much of which centred on Dublin. Changes in the pub industry have continued apace over recent decades. The 1980s witnessed the wider availability of food served in pubs with the first carveries in the city. Toasted sandwiches, crisps and peanuts were long the staple sustenance in many Dublin pubs but over the last few decades the march of the gastropub has been relentless. The 1990s ushered in an era of superpubs in the city to accommodate the increasing numbers of young people with high disposable income in the burgeoning economy. The first decade of the twenty-first century witnessed the cold winds of economic recession in Ireland and many pubs went to the wall, overexposed by bank loans and stung by dropping revenues. The increasing availability of home technologies, the smoking ban, strictly enforced drink-driving legislation and changing societal entertainment patterns have all posed significant threats to the industry. However, it has stabilised and recovered in recent years and the venerable institution of the Dublin pub looks like it will continue to thrive into the future, albeit, perhaps, under ever-evolving guises. The great Victorian heritage pubs will always endure but the specialist cocktail bars, craft beer houses, and increasingly sophisticated gastropubs will, most likely, form part of an ever-changing scene. Yet, as long as the core values of conviviality and hospitality continue to exist there will always be a place for the pub in Dublin. It should be celebrated and treasured in equal – and sensible – measure.

A Note on Licensing Laws

The subject of licensing laws in respect of public houses in Ireland is a vast one and a complete knowledge of the subject would test a great mind. The regulation opening hours (excluding late licences) now pertaining were legislated for in 2000, with some minor changes in 2003. Pubs can now open between 10.30 a.m. and 11.30 p.m. on Mondays, Tuesdays, Wednesdays and Thursdays; between 10.30 a.m. and 12.30 a.m. on Fridays and Saturdays; and between 12.30 p.m. and 11.30 p.m. on Sundays. On the eve of public holidays opening hours can be extended by an hour. Up until 2000 there were distinctions made between 'summer' and 'not summer' opening hours, whereby pubs had to close a half hour earlier during the latter period. 2017 was the last year on which pubs in the Republic of Ireland were required to stay closed on Good Friday. Christmas Day is now the only day on which pubs by law must keep their doors shut. Until 1943 Sunday was a closed day.

Dublin City Centre South

1. The Bailey

1-4 Duke Street, Dublin 2, 01 6704939, www.baileybarcafe.com

'The light music of whiskey falling into a glass ... an agreeable interlude'

James Joyce

Before 1705 the area of Dublin where the Bailey pub now stands was nothing more than a marsh, lacking even a proper road crossing. Joshua Dawson, after whom the nearby upmarket Dawson Street is named, changed that when he started to develop the area for residential purposes to accommodate the expanding population of the city. Before long, it became a highly desirable location to reside and do business in. Joshua built himself a fine residence on Dawson Street – but unfortunately never got to live in it – which is now the Mansion House, the home of the Lord Mayor of Dublin.

In 1837 John Bailey established an oyster bar on the site where the Bailey now stands, and advertisements from the time mention 'hot joints of beef and oyster for a shilling' – products firmly aimed at the upper end of the market. The bar even provided takeout and delivery services for those who could afford it. In keeping with its upmarket leanings the venue became a haunt of man-about-town Oliver St John Gogarty. Gogarty, an eminent writer, throat surgeon and social gadfly, reckoned the bar had 'the best whiskey and the best beefsteak in Dublin' and was the 'true museum' of the city. Charles Stewart Parnell, the so-called 'Uncrowned King of Ireland', leader of the Irish Party in the House of Commons and promoter of Irish Home Rule, was so well thought of by the owners that he was given his own room upstairs, where he discussed political strategy and planned for Ireland's future; it became known as 'Parnell's smoking room'. When the esteemed politician was in Dublin he stayed in a hotel on nearby Dawson Street and the Bailey became his de facto office.

In the early years of the twentieth century nationalist poets Thomas Kettle and Padraic Colum both frequented the bar, as did the founder of Sinn Féin, Arthur Griffith – indicative of the political sympathies of the owners. Kettle was a lieutenant in the Royal Irish Fusiliers and was later killed at Ginchy during the course of the First World War; he once famously wrote that 'Ireland could only become truly Irish if she first became European', a view ahead of his time except, perhaps, for a few fellow writers like James Joyce and Samuel Beckett.

Griffith, an ardent scholar of political history and committed republican, often spent his evenings in the Bailey after reading at the nearby National Library on Kildare Street. During the course of the Anglo-Irish Treaty negotiations Winston Churchill, a man famous for his caustic wit, commented that Griffith was 'an unusual figure, a silent Irishman'.

In 1957 John Ryan bought the Bailey and this change of ownership coincided with a new golden age for the pub. Ryan was a key figure in artistic and cultural circles in 1940s' and 1950s' Dublin. He founded the influential journal *Envoy: A Review of Literature and Art*, and, as well as working as a publican, was an artist, broadcaster, critic and editor. Ryan was a friend and benefactor of a number of struggling writers who regularly attended his pub, including Patrick Kavanagh, Brendan Behan, J.P. Donleavy and Flann O'Brien. It was Ryan who first published Brendan Behan's short stories and employed Kavanagh to write his infamously scurrilous monthly 'Diary' in *Envoy* magazine.

Behan even made some notes in the margins of the text of the late Donleavy's novel *The Gingerbread Man* in the Bailey one night which the author later incorporated into the text. After a theatrical version of *The Gingerbread Man* was pulled from the stage of the Gaiety Theatre after only one show – largely because the Catholic hierarchy objected – a group of literati and thespians held a wake in the Bailey.

John Ryan was an early admirer of James Joyce and he – and the Bailey – played a crucial role in preserving a significant item of Joycean heritage. In the mid-1960s some of the houses on Eccles Street, including No. 7, were partly demolished to prepare the site for the construction of a new wing of the Mater Private Hospital. The door was historically and culturally important because it was the fictional home of Leopold Bloom, of *Ulysses* fame. John Ryan recognised the significance of the address and set about preserving of it. Along with poet Patrick Kavanagh, novelist Flann O'Brien and others, he entered into negotiations to purchase the door of the house from the nuns who owned the land. Apparently the negotiations nearly came to a halt when the reverend mother learned of the building's association with 'that pagan writer'. Fortunately, Ryan was able to negotiate a settlement and the door was installed in the Bailey, where Patrick Kavanagh declared it officially 'shut' on Bloomsday, 16 June 1967.

Sadly, Brendan Behan did not live to see the day but his death had been noted in the Bailey three years earlier, according to John Ryan. On the day of Behan's death Ryan visited the terminally ill writer in Meath Street Hospital and afterwards returned to his pub:

> We made our way back to the Bailey. The clans had begun to gather and the drinks to flow. A period of great conviviality, never long separated from death among the Irish, was now imminent .... At six o'clock, a 'phone call' came from the Meath. Yes, all was well now. Brendan Behan had died peacefully. He had just turned forty.

While alive Behan was wont to tell a likely story concerning himself and the pub. He claimed that he once bought the pub by mistake at an auction in 1955 when he was merely making a bid on an electric toaster. No documentary proof of this transaction exists.

John Ryan passed away in 1992 at the age of 67, after a lifetime spent supporting the arts in Ireland.

The Bailey was part of the Brown Thomas building bought in 1994 by Marks and Spencer, and the problem of what to do with the door arose once again. It was eventually solved when it was moved to the newly established James Joyce Centre at North Great George's Street, where it still resides.

The Bailey is now a leading light in the Joycean heritage industry. Well-heeled tourists gather around the long counter to sample the gourmet food on offer, and the most elevated of Dublin's social circle are as welcome here as they were in the pub's original incarnation. The pub is renowned for seafood and is particularly well known for its Guinness and oysters. The outside heated patio area is one of the city's prime people-watching points. Appropriately, the Bailey continues to be at the centre of Bloomsday celebrations every year.

The First Bloomsday

The first Bloomsday was organised by John Ryan and Flann O'Brien in 1954 to commemorate the fiftieth anniversary of the famous journey taken around Dublin by Leopold Bloom on 16

June 1904 in James Joyce's *Ulysses*. It was also the day Joyce met Nora Barnacle, the love of his life. Ryan and O'Brien were joined by Patrick Kavanagh, Anthony Cronin, Tom Joyce (a dentist and cousin of James) and A.J. Leventhal (a lecturer in French in Trinity College Dublin). They hired two horse-drawn cabs – chosen because Leopold Bloom had attended Paddy Dignam's funeral in a similar vehicle in the novel – and assumed the roles of various characters from the novel. They first went to visit the Martello tower in Sandymount where Joyce had once lived for a short period. The men had envisioned a trip around the city during the daytime to visit different scenes from the novel, and planned to end up later in the evening in what had once been a red-light district which Joyce called 'Nighttown'. Unfortunately, as can the nature of these things in the convivial atmosphere of the Irish pub, the participants did not get past the Bailey, where they had decided to stop for a drink after an invitation from proprietor and participant John Ryan. He recounted proceedings in his book of reminiscences, *Remembering How We Stood* – renamed *Remember How We Staggered* by some Dublin wits. Despite the limited achievements of its first iteration Bloomsday subsequently went from strength to strength, and is now an eagerly anticipated part of the city's annual social calendar.

2. The Bank Bar and Restaurant

20-22 College Green, Dublin 2, 01 6770677,
www.bankoncollegegreen.com

The Bank Bar and Restaurant on College Green is located across the street from what once the most important political nerve centre of the city of Dublin. Grattan's Parliament (now the Bank of Ireland) was the first purpose-built parliament house in the world. The original building, designed by Edward Pearce, was constructed between 1729 and 1739, and formed only part of the now existing structure. The beautiful east portico – the then entrance to the House of Lords – was added by James Gandon between 1785 and 1787. The parliament of eighteenth-century Ireland was largely controlled by the wealthy Protestant Ascendancy, and on 2 August 1800 voted itself out of existence through the Act of Union. With the passing of the Act of Union the centre of power shifted to London, and with it the desire for improvements to Dublin as many of the ascendancy chose to stay in Britain when not in residence on their Irish country estates. Afterwards Dublin began a slow slide into disrepair and decay, and many once-great houses were split up into tenements for the urban poor. The parliament building was eventually sold to the Bank of Ireland under the condition that it should not be used for political assemblies.

The imposing Victorian building which now houses the Bank Bar and Restaurant was bought by the Belfast Bank in 1892 from British Mutual and, over the course of two years and at a cost of over £8,000, was modified into an impressive financial house under the watchful eye of architect William Henry Lynn. In 1966 the Belfast Bank and the Royal Bank merged to form Allied Irish Banks, the largest in Ireland. There is still a sign for the Royal Bank immediately inside the front door. The original vaults and Chatwood safes are still on display, as are the beautiful stained glass windows, mosaic-tiled floors, and hand-carved plasterwork and cornicing. The exterior of the building is considered Franco-Scottish and one of the rare examples of Scottish sandstone in the city. The office which once housed the director of the bank is now a beautiful snug. The late sports journalist Con Houlihan is commemorated by a bust in the front of the premises, an appropriate location given his predilection for the pleasures of the public house. The Bank opened as a bar and restaurant in 2003 and is now owned by serial publican Charlie Chawke. For the visitor enjoying the delights of the nearby shopping areas or the number of historical sites in the immediate area this establishment makes for a good place to stop and have something to drink and eat in exceptional architectural surroundings. For the reluctant tourist there is even an exact replica of the *Book of Kells* behind the bar, obviating the need to join the queue at nearby Trinity College to see the real thing.

3. The Bar With No Name

3 Fade Street, Dublin 2, 087 1221064, nonamebardublin.com

This newcomer is recognisable by the large wooden snail hanging above the door on fashionable Fade Street. Despite the name, this hip establishment is anything but secret and has acquired a significant reputation for its brunch offerings and highly regarded mojitos. If sparsely decorated spaces with achingly hip patrons is on the visitor's wish list then this could fit the bill. It could be New York, Tokyo or Paris. The rooftop terrace, complete with heated circus top covering, is a thing of beauty, and an incredibly popular gathering point for young urbanites. With the eclectic mix of Helmut Newton photographs on the walls and the extremely comfortable couches this is a bar in the vanguard of the very newest dispensation. It is very busy at weekend nights.

The 'Holy Hour'

Until 1988 pubs in Dublin and Cork had to observe a weekday 'holy hour' closure between 2.30 p.m. and 3.30 p.m. This ruling had been abolished for all other pubs in the country in 1962. The much discussed, and sometimes mythologised, 'holy hour' had endured since it was introduced by Minister Kevin O'Higgins during the early years of the newly independent country, ostensibly in an effort to make sure workers returned to their workplace after a liquid lunch. The enforced closing order became known as 'holy' because, some say, the only place for the martyred drinker to go during the hour was the nearest church. (In reality the objective of many a seasoned drinker was to find a public house where they could obtain a 'lock-in' for the designated non-drinking time.) In his history of the Licensed Vintners' Association (LVA), Eamon Casey referred to the comments of a British trade union official who once visited Dublin and saw the whole business in action: 'The Irish love to acclaim the 1913 Lockout but they should really acclaim the great lock-in each afternoon in Dublin's pubs.' It is an era of Irish social and cultural history that has long come to an end, though the 'holy hour' still features prominently in the public imagination.

4. The Bernard Shaw

11-12 Richmond Street South, Saint Kevin's, Dublin 2, 01 9060218, www.thebernardshaw.com

In an unlikely-to-be-intended irony this pub is now frequented by hipsters with beards almost, but in the vast majority of cases not, as impressive as that of the great writer George Bernard Shaw himself.

This pub would have been as alien to the great playwright as the far side of Jupiter. A big blue bus parked in the backyard selling highly regarded pizza, a flea market in the same space on the first and third Saturday of every month, yoga sessions, table tennis and beer pong tables, a projector screen, craft beers of every hue and colour, a wide choice of cocktails, occasional art shows, graffiti-covered walls, home-brew championships – all are part of this brave new hipster world. No eminent Victorian publican could have come up with this version of a public house in their wildest dreams. The Bernard Shaw has a vast beer garden and, when the weather is right, the mass of humanity here is a sight to behold. Niall Harbison of website *Loving' Dublin* has written a superlative description of this one-of-a-kind pub: 'It can best be described as an eclectic mix of a

Berlin nightclub, old Dublin bar, and Amsterdam coffee shop with an outdoor art gallery thrown in for the craic. The place is absolutely mental .... Whoever designed this place wasn't just on drugs but probably at the peak of a 6-day crack bender.'

5. The Bleeding Horse

24-25 Upper Camden Street, Dublin 2, 01 4752705, www. bleedinghorse.ie

Dating back to the seventeenth century – the current building is recorded as having being built in 1871 – this pub is located at what was once an important junction of two main routes leading out of the city: Charlotte Street led to Ranelagh and Donnybrook on one side, while Old Camden Street joined Richmond Street and led to Rathmines and Cullenswood on the other. Both old street names disappeared during renovations in the 1990s. There are conflicting stories as to how this venerable pub got its intriguing name. One suggests it was because horses were once bled by farriers when they got fits or 'staggers'. Alternatively, the name may be inspired by an incident in the Battle of Rathmines in 1649 when a wounded horse fled the scene of battle and entered the pub, the basis of a frequently cited ghost story. This narrative suggests the unfortunate rider was

shot dead, while the horse was severely wounded and wandered around the area looking for a place to lie down, before spying the open doors of the pub. Stumbling in, the horse fell to the floor and died, leaving a large blood stain on the floor. Legend says that this stain is still on the floor behind the bar on the first floor, and that the horse's spirit now haunts the pub during the small hours of the morning, when noises and commotion can be heard from the front room.

Whatever about the origins of the name, the literary pedigree of the Bleeding Horse is very impressive, having once been frequented by Irish mystical poet James Clarence Mangan, amongst others. Mangan's life was blighted by opium and alcohol addiction, and it was only after his death that he became recognised as a major poet for haunting works such as 'Dark Rosaleen' and 'A Vision of Connaught in the Thirteenth Century'.

The Bleeding Horse also features in Sheridan Le Fanu's novel *The Cock and Anchor* (1845). Le Fanu, best known for his Victorian ghost stories, described the pub in the opening passage of his thriller thus:

A small, old-fashioned building, something between an alehouse and an inn. It occupied the roadside by no means unpicturesquely; one gable jutted into the road, with a projecting window, which stood out from the building like a glass box held together by a massive frame of wood; and commanded by this projecting gable, and a few yards in retreat, but facing the road, was the inn door, over which hung a painted panel, representing a white horse, out of whose neck there spouted a crimson cascade, and underneath, in large letters, the traveller was informed that this was the genuine old 'Bleeding Horse'.

The observant pub scholar will notice an engraved stone panel on the side entrance of the pub commemorating Le Fanu's work, which simply reads 'Two horsemen rode to the ... Bleeding Horse, Joseph Sheridan Le Fanu, *The Cock and Anchor*'.

The pub also features in *Ulysses* when Leopold Bloom considered the (vague) possibility of getting a job there: 'I saw him a few times in the Bleeding Horse in Camden Street with Boylan the billsticker.

You might put in a good word for us to get me taken on there.' He did not get it. A story has long circulated that James Joyce was once thrown out of the premises when he was caught looking up the skirt of an actress after falling down the stairs drunk.

During the 1960s the pub traded as the Falcon for a number of years, but reverted to the original name in the early 1970s. The interior of the Bleeding Horse was renovated in 1992 in the contemporary faux Victorian style of the modern period, and was extended over three floors to cater for the increasingly diverse community living in this part of Dublin city. It may not be the most exciting destination in this part of town but the large windows allow for excellent people-watching. The scooped-out centre and overhanging mezzanines provide a large space and, unusually for an Irish pub, this venue tends to fill from the bottom up.

A Dublin Pub in the Nineteenth Century

Madame Marie-Anne De Bovet, a French traveller who recorded her thoughts in *Three Months in Ireland*, is one of the very few writers who described the inside of an Irish pub in the nineteenth century – and even then she only looked in the window. Madame De Bovet was travelling by carriage through the streets of nighttime Dublin in 1890 when she noticed 'a great flare of gas, accompanied with the sound of voices'. It was a public house, of which she was very disapproving. The people, she wrote, looked poor and miserable, 'huddled together like a flock of sheep'. They were all standing about, leaning on the counter or up against the wall, in an 'atmosphere poisoned by alcoholic vapours, thick with tobacco smoke, and reeking with the exhalations of foul humanity ... the noise an eternal Sabbath'. She observed the landlord removing some of the inebriates with the help of the few sober customers. These wretches, she wrote, 'stagger away to their hovels, to sleep off the fumes of the whiskey, provided that before this they had not already tumbled down in some corner, there to snore till morning'. She noted both men and women in the pub, and, while she found a drunken man distasteful, it was nothing compared to the sight of an inebriated woman. Her sensibilities were further damaged when a drunken woman was thrown out into the street beside her carriage: 'It is a hideous spectacle – this miserable emaciated creature; her gaunt limbs which tremble convulsively are hardly covered by her dirty rags; her eye is fixed, and she has the mad look of a wild beast, having been brutally jostled by the sneering crowd.' What would she make of Temple Bar?

6. Bowe's

31 Fleet Street, Dublin 2, 01 6714038,
www.bowespub.com

'This pub is dedicated to those merry souls who make drinking a pleasure, who reach contentment before capacity, and what so ever they drink, can hold it and remain gentlemen.'
Sign behind the bar in Bowe's of Fleet Street

Bowe's does not immediately come to mind when the great Victorian pubs of Dublin are considered but, in its own quiet way, it is a fine example of the beauty inherent in the remaining premises that qualify for membership of this exclusive club. When it first opened in 1854, under the steward-ship of Christopher McCabe, it was both pub and lodging house, while the next owner, John Walsh, owned the College Hotel directly behind Bowe's as well as the pub. The fixtures and fittings now extant date to the great Victorian pub-building boom between 1880 and 1890, by which time the premises had come under the ownership of John O'Connor. The two-faced clock is a particular rarity in the city as it still has to be wound manually each day.

Bowe's had a role to play in the 1916 Easter Rising – which eventually led to Irish independence – when it was commandeered by militants but quickly evacuated after their position came under attack. In their haste some of the rebels left their weapons behind, bravely retrieved by members of Cumann na mBan, as described by Annie O'Brien:

Word came in from a sniping post, a public house called Bowe's at the corner of William St and Coppinger Row, that the two snipers at that post had evacuated it, leaving their arms behind them, and they sent word to Dawson St to have their arms collected and put into safe keeping. The two of us went to the post and found the house locked up. We went to the house next door where we found a friendly man who showed us up to the skylight which we got through and on to the roof of the public house. Its skylight was a bit small and only my sister, who was small, was able to get through. She went down and opened the door of the public house for the rest of us. We had to search the whole of the house for the arms and at last we found the two loaded rifles in an office.

Bowe's was a long-time favourite for staff of the *Irish Times* newspaper, which once had its offices in nearby D'Olier Street – hence the oft-used term 'The Old Lady of D'Olier Street' to describe the august media organ.

At the height of the Victorian era in 1895 the pub was owned by James Rochford, whose name can still be seen on mirrors inside the bar and on the end wall on the outside of the building, while there are also bottles with Rochford's name on show inside the pub. It was 1920 before the name Bowe came to the premises, when James Bowe took charge, one of a family who owned a number of pubs in the city at that time, including the now Grogan's Castle Lounge.

Like a number of other Dublin pubs, Bowe's has developed a highly regarded whiskey bar in recent years. The Irish Whiskey Appreciation Society was founded in Bowe's pub but has since moved on. When eminent pub authority Gary Quinn visited the pub for his excellent 'Barfly' column in the *Irish Times* in 2016 there were a grand total of 227 varieties of whiskey on offer.

The stained glass in the front window may at first confuse patrons and passers-by due to its resemblance to a map of Africa but is, in fact, a map of the Irish county of Carlow – home of the current owner, Declan Doyle. Bowe's is an oasis of calm in this frenetic part of the city, and is a wonderful location to take a break from shopping on the nearby O'Connell, Henry and Mary Streets. A fine feather was added to Bowe's cap with the publication of *Straight Up: The Insiders' Guide to the World's Most Interesting Bars and Drinking Experiences (2017)* by Joel Harrison and Neil Ridley. The authors of the book described Bowe's as 'The Emerald of Dublin' and recommended a pint of Guinness, adding, 'Bowe's imbues a sense of Irish hospitality into the wonderful surroundings of a traditional Victorian-style Irish boozer'. This pub comes highly recommended.

Easter Rising 1916 and Dublin Pubs

The Easter Rising took place in Dublin between Monday 24 April and Sunday 29 April 1916. It was a rebellion against British rule in Ireland and was defeated after a swift military response. As a military campaign the 1916 Rising was a failure but the British response to the event eventually changed the course of Irish history. The execution of the leaders turned many people away from the idea of Home Rule through political negotiation and towards the concept of a fully independent Irish Republic by armed insurrection.

The Irish rebels began their action by seizing the General Post Office (GPO) and adjacent buildings in the city centre on Easter Monday morning. Bowe's was not the only pub in Dublin to see action during that fateful week. The owner of nearby Mooney's public house would not allow the rebels access and, despite firing a shot at the door lock, they failed to gain ingress. Undaunted, the militants proceeded to the nearby Ship Tavern where they found a friendlier reception. Unfortunately, the pub was later destroyed by British bombing. J.T. Davy's pub in Portobello, on the route between Rathmines Barracks and the city centre, was also commandeered by rebel forces. There they planned to disrupt the movement of British troops towards the fighting zone by using the premises as a sniping location. In this they were successful. Delahunt's pub on Camden Street was seized on Easter Monday night by rebels, aided by republican-minded barman George Heuston. A little further down the street, opposite Jacob's factory, the Swan pub was also commandeered. Philip Little's pub was seized on Monday night by forces retreating from the by-then abandoned Davy's pub.

On the north side of the city O'Reilly's on North King Street – now the Tap pub – was seized by the rebels to slow the progress of the British troops from the Royal Barracks. Lambe's on Richmond Road – now Meagher's of Ballybough – was taken by another group of rebels attempting to halt the advance of British troops from a training camp on Bull Island towards the centre of the city. The Irish brigade held Lambe's until they were ordered to fall back to the GPO.

The British Army also saw the benefits of the strategic use of pubs and seized Egan's in Smithfield to use as a firing position on Church Street and North King Street.

By the end of the week's skirmishing the collateral damage suffered by the city's hostelries was substantial. Some of the pubs completely destroyed or severely damaged as a result of fire from both sides included Mooney's, McGreevy's and Moore's on Eden Quay; J. Humphrey's and Fee's on Moore Street; Farrell's of Marlborough Street; Kavanagh's on Lower Bridgefoot Street; the Oval on Abbey Street; and the famous Brazen Head on the city quays.

7. The Brazen Head

20 Lower Bridge Street, Merchant's Quay, Dublin 8, 01 6795186,
www.brazenhead.com

Just a stone's throw from the home of Guinness at Saint James's Gate sits the Brazen Head, a pub which claims to be the oldest in Ireland. This, in certain quarters, is a matter of some heated debate.

The Brazen Head claims to date back to 1198. The gates of the old Norman city were once located here, and were closed at night to keep 'foreigners' out – at that time the foreigners were the native Irish. There were many taverns in the area to accommodate those who had to leave the city, or those who stayed outside before entering to conduct their business the following day, and it is claimed the Brazen Head was one such establishment. The owners of the pub were once challenged to a debate on national radio by the owners of Seán's Bar in Athlone, County Westmeath to decide which of their establishments should be recognised as the oldest pub in Ireland. The owners of Seán's
Bar provided evidence in the form of clay-and-wattle samples from a wall (verified by archaeologists and historians from the National Museum by carbon dating) which suggested the presence of a retail premises on the site dating back to AD 900, and were awarded the title. They also provided tavern tokens to add further substance to their claim. Although there were similar tokens found at nearby Winetavern Street when Dublin Corporation controversially exca-vated the nearby Wood Quay site in the 1980s, there was nothing to connect them to the Brazen Head. Guinness World Records accepted this decision and duly recorded Seán's Bar as the oldest in Ireland. The Brazen Head may have taken some consolation when a signa-ture etched on a window was confirmed to be from 1726 and was awarded the title of the oldest piece of graffiti in the country. The writing – in a whorl on a bottle-glass pane – is so small it cannot be read with the naked eye but with the aid of a magnifying glass it is just about possible to decipher that 'John Langan halted here 7th August 1726.'

While the overall trajectory of the development of this famous pub is fraught with some foggy details the arguments are intriguing.

According to some historians the pub may have appropriated the name from a nearby building called the Brazen Lady, and the building now standing may have been constructed in the mid-seventeenth century. The oldest documentation the owners provided for the radio debate was a court certificate of ownership from 1613, noting there was a pub here belonging to Richard and Eleanor Fagan at that time. The Fagans were landed gentry with extensive holdings in Dublin, Meath, Sligo and parts of Munster. There is also a licence for the pub dating from 1668, just after the restoration of King Charles II to the British crown.

Historial records name a number of different owners of the Brazen Head over the centuries. During the tenure of Denis Mitchell, the United Irishmen reputedly held meetings on the premises and it has been claimed that Oliver Bond, one of the prominent members of the organisation, outlined his plans for the capture of Dublin at one such gathering. Additionally, it has been suggested that the leader of the group, Robert Emmet, hid out here after the failed rising of 1803 and that he still haunts the premises. Some sources suggest Emmet actually lived here for a while, renting a room that overlooked the passageway leading to the door of the inn, from where all callers could be observed. His writing table was even once on display in the pub. Emmet is most remembered for his stirring speech from the dock before his execution: 'When my country takes her place among the nations of the earth, then, and only then, let my epitaph be written.'

In earlier times the Brazen Head was frequented by satirical writer and dean of the nearby Saint Patrick's Cathedral Jonathan Swift, while there are even rumours that Robin Hood once paused here for a libation.

The stories behind the name of the pub are equally interesting. One suggests that a stray cannon 'removed the head of a well-known red-haired girl of ill repute' during the Williamite wars of 1689–1691. According to the narrative she had been watching the nearby skirmish from the window of her brothel when the misfortune befell her. When the new tavern was built on the location in 1750 it was called 'The Sign of the Brazen Head'. If that sounds too dramatic, an alternative rendering of the origin may be more credible. In late medieval times an all-knowing figure embodied in the shape of a bronze or brass head with the ability to answer any question put to it was a frequent literary motif. This font of wisdom was known to literary scholars as the 'Brazen Head'.

In later times the insurrectionists of 1916 and the leaders of the War of Independence are said to have gathered here for meetings to plan revolution, while other patriots who may have crossed the threshold include Theobald Wolfe Tone and Daniel O'Connell.

James Joyce mentioned the pub in *Ulysses* when Leopold Bloom referenced the food. Bloom's associate McConachie informed him he could get 'a decent enough do in the Brazen Head over in Wine-tavern Street'. For once Joyce got the address wrong – it was on Bridge Street then too.

In more modern times it was another of the many premises in the city graced – and sometimes disgraced – by the boisterous presence of writers Brendan Behan and Flann O'Brien.

Whatever about the exact provenance of the building it is hard not to feel like stepping back in time when passing through the castel-lated gate. The dark-beamed interior further enhances the historical atmosphere. The Brazen Head is a popular venue for traditional Irish music, a fact emphasised by a sign in the bar which reads 'Only traditional Irish music allowed in this bar', although Van Morrison, Paolo Nutini and Tom Jones have all played here over the years, and none could be accused of being staunch traditional Irish musicians. The Brazen Head continues to go from strength to strength and is more on the tourist trail than ever.

8. Bruxelles

7-8 Harry Street, Dublin 2, 01 6775362, www.bruxelles.ie

The pub that is now Bruxelles was known as the Zodiac Lounge when it first opened for business in 1886. James G. Mooney bought No. 7 Harry Street in 1885, and the following year he purchased No. 8. No. 7 had previously housed one of Dublin's first gin palaces, called Duvall's. The Zodiac Lounge was part of a group of pubs owned by the Mooney family, and was sometimes referred to as the Grafton

Mooney; its sister pub, Parnell Heritage Pub on Parnell Street, was known as the Parnell Mooney.

The Zodiac Lounge was designed and built by Dublin architect J.J. O' Callaghan, known primarily for his gothic-inspired work: the round tower with the distinctive winding staircase inside the pub is an excellent example of this impressive style. In the latter part of the nineteenth century there was a revival of interest in spiritual and supernatural phenomena; the ancient pastimes of astrology and horoscopes came back into vogue, and mosaic representations of the zodiac were not uncommon in public buildings – 130-year-old tiled mosaic figures representing the twelve star signs are still to be seen behind the main bar here. The current owners, the Egan family, bought the pub in the early 1970s at the same time Ireland was joining the European Economic Community (EEC) (now the European Union (EU)). It was an era of hope and expectation in Ireland as most people looked to the EEC to solve persistent economic problems in the country after its accession in 1973. With this posi-tivity and sense of Europeanisation the owners named the pub after the Belgian capital where the central administration of the European Community was, and is, based. All the flags of the member states hang from the roof of the bar, added to as the union expanded over the years to its now 28-country membership (including the soon-to-depart Britain). Visitors from North America may be put out that their much-loved flags are not on display, but there is no hidden agenda here.

Bruxelles is synonymous with the Irish rock music scene, most particularly with Phil Lynott. From the late 1960s the Grafton Mooney – as it was known until 1973 – was the haunt of Lynott and members of his band, Thin Lizzy, as well as Brush Shiels and his band, Skid Row, amongst others. While the nearby McDaid's pub accommodated the folk singers the more rock-orientated performers gravitated to the Grafton Mooney. In a monochromatic Ireland, Lynott, who had a black father, was an exotic addition to Dublin culture. He lived up to the image of the rock star given to excess, and eventually succumbed to septicaemia after a prolonged bout of drinking and drug-taking in 1986 at the young age of 36. Lynott had a hugely successful, but tragically short, musical career. The pub is a Mecca for those fans seeking to commune with his spirit and it is not unusual to meet fans of his music from the most remote corners of the earth. There is a substantial amount of memorabilia, much of it donated by the singer's mother, Philomena, in the Flanders Lounge section, and a beautiful Phil Lynott snug at the back of the premises. In case the association between the pub and Lynott is missed, there is a statue of 'Philo', as he is widely referred to by his legion of admirers, outside the pub. The Paul Daly sculpture has been damaged twice since it was erected in 2005 by the Roisín Dubh Trust, established to commemorate Lynott's life. In 2013 vandals knocked it off its plinth and in 2015 the guitar was knocked out of the singer's hands by a passing motorist, but, in true rock-and-roll style, it was repaired each time.

Over the years Bruxelles has seen a galaxy of rock stars cross its threshold, including Iron Maiden, AC/DC, Anthrax, Journey, Axl Rose and Slash of Guns N' Roses, and Ronnie Wood of the Rolling Stones. Michael Flatley, the star of Riverdance, once danced on the bar, while Bruce Springsteen called in unannounced for a pint on his own one day. American actors Alec Baldwin and Kim Basinger had lunch on Saint Stephen's Day one year – and later named their daughter Ireland – while American folk singer John Denver had a pint there, only a week before his tragic death in an airplane crash in Colorado. It was also the unofficial headquarters of the cast and crew of the hugely successful 1997 Alan Parker film *The Commitments*, based on the 1987 novel of the same name by Roddy Doyle, which told the story of a motley group of Dubliners and their quest to make it as a successful soul band.

What Not to Order in a Dublin Pub: The 'Irish Car Bomb'

The wildly politically incorrectly named 'Irish car bomb' is an American cocktail made with Irish stout, Irish cream liqueur and Irish whiskey, and was reputedly invented in 1979 by owner Charles Oat at Wilson's Saloon in Norwich, Connecticut. The double entendre is as subtle as the drink itself. It is a 'bomb shot', and an obvious reference to the car bombs once synonymous with the Troubles in Northern Ireland. It is not advisable to go into any Irish pub in Ireland and ask for one. This is particularly the case in Dublin where a number of pubs were targeted in the 1970s during the height of the Troubles. The inclusion of the drink in the promotional material of an English bar in 2014 drew widespread complaints and caused public outrage, resulting in a withdrawal of the offending promotional flyers and a public apology by the bar manager.

To make the drink, whiskey (Jameson preferably) is floated on top of Irish cream liqueur (Baileys if you have it) in a shot glass, and the shot glass is then dropped into the stout – inevitably Guinness. Once mixed, it must be consumed quickly or else .... It brings a whole new meaning to the phrase 'getting bombed'. All in all, it is best left in the United States.

9. Cafe en Seine

Cafe en Seine, 40 Dawson Street, Dublin 2, 01 6774567,
www.cafeenseine.ie

With its art deco interior, three-storey glass atrium with forty-foot-high trees, huge lanterns, a lift imported from a French hotel

running between the three floors, real twelve-metre-high trees, beautiful soft flocked wallpaper, a grand piano and umpteen statues, including an impressive Louis XIV bust among them, this is, as this bar likes to say, 'a little bit of Paris in Dublin'. It is a big space but still seems intimate. Cafe en Seine is certainly a world removed from the image of a traditional Irish pub. If you have the money this plush establishment is likely to have the product. A cool bottle of Cristal champagne with a selection of mixers can be brought to your table for €400. After 10 p.m. Cafe en Seine mutates into a nightclub.

The building housing the pub has had a colourful and wide-ranging history. After the failed rising of 1798 French prisoners were housed here. One of those incarcerated is reputed to have been a six-foot-tall woman who later became the inspiration for the Statue of Liberty. In the nineteenth century the building became home to a high-class bordello which reputedly numbered King George IV among its clients. Subsequently it was occupied by a dressmaker called Mrs Russell who once, the story goes, made a dress for Queen Victoria. Apart from those illustrious royal connections the vener-able building variously housed a clerical club, a doctor's surgery, a bicycle shop, a piano warehouse and a car showroom. Even the Irish government resided here for a short period.

When the super-pub boom hit Ireland in the 1990s Cafe en Seine was the most ostentatious of those built when it opened its doors in 1995. The lavish decor – reputedly the most expensive makeover ever on an Irish pub – reflects the genteel nature of the neighbourhood, located as it is in the heart of where Ireland's decision-makers go about their daily business. In 2015 Cafe en Seine was voted Dublin's City Bar of the Year.

After an extensive five-month makeover costing €4 million Cafe en Seine reopened its doors in November 2018. It now feels even more Parisian with its brasserie, indoor–outdoor 'street garden' complete with retractable roof, pastiche shopfronts, pop-up art gallery, coffee shop and a bar counter with a period building façade as a backdrop. There are even 'mummified' trees to enhance the sense of being on a terraced bar in downtown Paris, and there are no fewer than seven distinct eating and drinking areas in these sprawling premises. The discerning customer is spoiled for choice; apart from the street garden there is a library area stocked with vintage hardbacks and comfortable armchairs, a cocktail bar and a 50-seater restaurant (with a separate entrance off Dawson Street). The upper floors house the Balcony Bar and the Loft Bar. The overall capacity is a staggering 1,100 people. This is the brave new world of the ever-expanding capital of Ireland and still home to the beautiful people.

10. Cassidy's

*42 Lower Camden Street, Dublin 2, 01 4746540, www.facebook.com/ pages/category/Pub/Cassidys-Pub-Camden-Street-3403163761692*39

When US President Bill Clinton came to Dublin in 1995 he was taken to this beautiful Victorian pub established in 1891 (although some sources, including the pub's website, suggest 1856) because he was, it was claimed, distantly related to the owners. His mother's maiden name was Virginia Dell Cassidy, and her roots dated back five generations to Levi Cassidy of Chesterfield, South Carolina. Bill Clinton spoke about his heritage in a speech at College Green in the city centre: 'My mother was a Cassidy and how I wish she were alive to be here with me today. She would have loved the small towns and she would have loved Dublin. Most of all, she would have loved the fact that in Ireland, you have nearly 300 racing days a year. She loved the horses.' Given her predispositions to the good things in life it is likely that Mrs Dell Cassidy would have also enjoyed a tipple in these beautiful premises if she had the opportunity.

The building now housing Cassidy's was once the home of the *Freeman's Journal*, the oldest nationalist paper in Ireland and spawning ground for some of those involved in the Easter Rising of 1916. The paper was originally more identified with eighteenth-century Protestant patriot politicians Henry Grattan and Henry Flood after its founding by Charles Lucas in 1763, but in the nineteenth century it began to become aligned with nationalist elements and by the 1880s it was the main supporter of Charles Stewart Parnell and the Irish Parliamentary Party. After Parnell's fall from grace, when his affair with Kitty O'Shea was exposed, the paper was gradually overtaken in sales by more organised publications and it eventually merged with the *Irish Independent*. The printing machinery was destroyed in 1922 by the Anti-Treaty IRA faction, although the *Freeman's Journal* limped on until 1924. Until

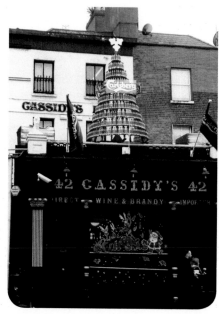

the 1990s the *Irish Independent* included the words 'incorporating the *Freeman's Journal*' in its mastheads and over its editorials. Famously, Leopold Bloom of *Ulysses* fame worked for the *Freeman's Journal* selling advertisements.

While the beautiful frontage of this pub, with its ornate gold lettering, might suggest a small, poky bar, this is far from the case. While there is a long thin bar at the bottom, there are now three floors in these unexpectedly extensive premises. In recent times Cassidy's has embraced the craft beer revolution and the popularity of board games. Many cite Cassidy's as serving the best Guinness in the city – a valued accolade in a tough competition. This pub has an atmosphere that is impossible to recreate and, with top-class traditional music frequently available, it should feature strongly on any itinerary taking in this part of the city.

US Presidents and Irish Pubs

It would seem that no visit to Ireland by a US president is complete without a visit to a hostelry to sample the delights on offer. Although John F. Kennedy did not get to a pub on his presidential tour of Ireland in 1963, he had visited Mulligan's pub on Poolbeg Street in 1947 as a cub journalist with the then news editor of the *Irish Press*, Jack Grealish. (Kennedy drank a bottle of lager.)

President Ronald Reagan visited his ancestral village of Ballyporeen, County Tipperary, in 1984 where he famously sipped a pint of Smithwick's in O'Farrell's pub with the world's media watching on. The bar was later renamed Ronald Reagan's in his honour. In June 2004 a member of the board of trustees of the Reagan Foundation visited Ballyporeen and found the pub closed and up for sale. He offered the owners $100,000 and the pub was moved in its entirety to the Ronald Reagan Museum in Simi, California, where it is now snugly located under the former presidential jet. Unfortunately, it does not sell any alcohol.

In 1983 George Bush Senior paid a visit to Ryan's of Parkgate Street while holding the office of Vice-President of the United States and, according to the pub's website, his son George W. Bush subsequently had a drink there too. A photograph in McGrattan's of Baggot Street, dating from 1996, shows Jimmy Carter and his wife in the dining room on a visit to Ireland. Bill Clinton also had the pleasure of accompanying the then Taoiseach (Irish Prime Minister) Bertie Ahern to his much-lauded local, Fagan's in Drumcondra, in 2000. (In keeping with his image of being a man of the people Ahern regularly had a pint in the pub when the notion took him.) In 2013 Barack Obama's wife Michelle and children visited Finnegan's pub in Dalkey in the august company of U2's Bono, while in 2011 the President was taken to Ollie Hayes' pub in the village of Moneygall on the Offaly-Tipperary border, from where his forefathers had set forth for the promised land. One American president who did not make it to an Irish pub would appear to have been Richard Nixon. Perhaps, in retrospect, this was wise, as Nixon was not complimentary towards the Irish on secretly recorded tapes, released after the Watergate scandal: 'The Irish have certain [traits] ... for example the Irish can't drink. What you always have to remember with the Irish is they get mean. Virtually every Irish I've known gets mean when he drinks ... particularly the real Irish.'

11. Davy Byrne's

21 Duke Street, Dublin 2, 01 6775217,
https://davybyrnes.com/

'The moral pub'

James Joyce, *Ulysses*

The origin of these celebrated premises can be traced back to 25 March 1722 when Richard Spain gave a lease on the farmland premises to Issac Eustaunie, a Jew whose family had migrated to Ireland during the eighteenth century. The original Davy Byrne came from the Wicklow Mountains to Dublin in 1863 where he found work as a barman. After spending sixteen years in the trade, during which time he first worked as an apprentice and then later as the manager of the famous Scotch House pub on Burgh Quay, he bought his own premises here

in 1889 from Matthew Riley for £2,300. He placed his name over the door, where it has remained ever since.

Of all the pubs in Dublin that claim literary significance through connections with James Joyce, it is Davy Byrne's that can point most directly and extensively to the written word. It is the famous 'moral pub' of *Ulysses* where Leopold Bloom, the central character in *Ulysses*, found solace on his ramble across Dublin: 'He entered Davy Byrne's. Moral pub. He doesn't chat. Stands a drink now and then. But in a leap year once in four. Cashed a cheque for me once.' This is from the famous 'Lestrygonians' episode in the novel. Bloom considered the publican an upright citizen because he did not bet, unlike so many of his associates. Nosey Flynn, a friend of Bloom's, had asked Byrne for a tip for the Gold Cup horse race in Ascot in England, but was politely dismissed:

> Davy Byrne came forward from the hindbar in tuckstitched shirtsleeves, cleaning his lips with two wipes of his napkin. Herring's blush. Whose smile upon each feature plays with such and such replete. Too much fat on the parsnips.
>
> - And here's himself and pepper on him, Nosey Flynn said. Can you give us a good one for the Gold cup?
> - I'm off that, Mr Flynn, Davy Byrne answered. I never put anything on a horse.
> - You're right there, Nosey Flynn said.

It is also in Davy Byrne's that Bloom partook of his celebrated lunch of a Gorgonzola cheese sandwich and a glass of wine, still available on the menu today. He had previously gone into the nearby (and now demolished) Burton restaurant and billiards room, but left in high disgust after he saw the lunchtime diners 'slopping in their stews and pints'. The food and atmosphere in Byrne's was more to his taste: 'Mr Bloom ate his strips of sandwich, fresh clean bread, with relish of disgust, pungent mustard, the feety savour of green cheese. Sips of his wine soothed his palate. Not logwood that. Tastes fuller this weather with the chill off. Nice quiet bar. Nice piece of wood in that counter. Nicely planed. Like the way it curves there.'

Apart from its connection with James Joyce, this pub has some other strong literary associations. Oliver St John Gogarty – the famous throat surgeon, writer and man about town – and author James Stephens – whom Joyce chose to finish his later novel *Finnegans Wake* – were known to partake of a drink here. Author and playwright Samuel Beckett, not a particular fan of pubs or Irish drinking habits, occasionally came here. The austere Beckett famously dismissed the 'indiscretion and broken glass' of the Dublin pub scene, and went on to find a much more agreeable social environment in the literary cafes of Paris.

In his brilliant book *Dead as Doornails* Anthony Cronin described an occasion when he witnessed Brendan Behan's ejection from the premises:

I was sitting by the counter in Davy Byrne's one evening when he came in. He stood a few yards away in the middle of the floor and delivered hoarsely of some well thought out if monotonous remarks about bogmen, Kulchies and the like. After a while I had enough and stood up ... but anyway at that moment the barman decided, somewhat reluctantly, to do their duty and he was shooled [sic] and persuaded off the premises, although such was their obvious nervousness, that it became a sort of whistle-stop tour, with Brendan making farewell addresses every few yards of the way.

Such is the literary pedigree of this fine establishment that Flann O'Brien once wrote that 'the premises bear openly the marks of their departed guests, like traces of fresh stout found in a glass by a policeman after hours'.

Davy Byrne's also claims a role in the birth of the Irish state. During the War of Independence, and the subsequent Civil War, it was frequented by many of the main players at the time. Davy Byrne was a nationalist sympathiser and allowed the upstairs to be used by the Irish Republican Brotherhood (IRB) and the outlawed Provisional Cabinet of the new Irish state, of which Michael Collins was Minister for Finance. A story is told of a barman trying to clear the bar with the time-honoured exhortation 'time gentlemen please' (this was a time when women were a rare presence in Irish pubs). A clued-in customer is said to have pithily replied: 'Time be damned! The Government is sitting upstairs.'

Having overseen the tumultuous political birth of the country, Byrne retired in 1939 and in 1942 the pub was bought by the Doran family of Marlbourgh Street, publicans of long standing. They modernised the building and Davy Byrne's was one of the first pubs to sell cocktails in the city.

The pub is now run by Redmond Doran and has acquired a reputation as a gastropub. It also houses some valuable art, including three murals of Joycean Dublin by Liam Proud, murals by Cecil Ffrench Salkeld (Brendan Behan's father-in-law) depicting life in 1940s' Dublin (located on the right-hand wall of the main bar), and sculptures by Eddie Delaney and John Behan behind the bar. The five figures in the sculptures represent the different branches of the creative arts: literature, music, painting, drama and science. The three murals by Salkeld are entitled *Morning*, *Noon* and *Evening*, and include depictions of playwright George Bernard Shaw, writer Flann O'Brien, and the much-lauded Irish Shakespearian actor Micheál Mac Liammóir.

There is also a beautiful art deco stained glass skylight, which throws a soft diffuse light over the area, adding further to the sense of being inside an art gallery. Along with the Bailey pub, immediately across the street, Davy Byrne's is ground zero for the annual Bloomsday celebrations and is a permanent part of the ever-expanding Joycean heritage industry.

If one asks nicely the barman may give you a copy of a famous photograph taken outside the pub on the first ever Bloomsday. The beautiful monochromatic image shows Patrick Kavanagh in louche repose on a pony trap with the more distant-looking Anthony Cronin evading the eye of the camera. The eventual location of the celebrants is still civilly disputed between Davy Byrne's and the Bailey but it matters none as both make more than an adequate living from proceedings.

Today Bloomsday is a much more elaborate affair, including liver and kidneys for breakfast, readings and re-enactments across the city, and, of course, the cheese and wine is still available in Byrne's.

12. Devitt's

78 Lower Camden Street, Saint Kevin's, Dublin 2, 01 4753414,
www.devittspub.ie

With the number 78 in large gold lettering on the red-bricked front,
and the blue-and-white canopy underneath, it would be virtually
impossible to miss this pub. This premises got an extensive makeover
in recent times, making what was a great pub even better according
to many connoisseurs. Devitt's is a brilliant example of a venerable
establishment being brought up to modern standards without
compromising the character or the integrity of the original premises.

The first licence issued for this premises in 1871 was taken out
by a Christopher C. Clinch, who traded as a tea, wine and spirit
merchant. At that time this was a prosperous area of Dublin city
where well-heeled Victorians resided. Clinch later added a grocery
section to his burgeoning business. In 1884 Clinch sold the business
on to Tipperary man Andrew Ryan, who in turn passed it on to
Patrick Ryan in 1890. This was the height of the Victorian era, and
Ryan was a successful businessman who also ran another public
house at No. 110 Thomas Street – a building of historical impor-
tance as it was the birth place of Power's Whiskey. When Jeremiah

Ahearne took over these premises in 1943 he was not to know the luck that would come his way when the Olympic Ballroom opened nearby in the early 1950s. It was a boon for his business and this became an exceptionally busy pub as the men went in beforehand to get some 'Dutch courage'. It was only in the 1970s that this premises acquired its current name when purchased by Limerick man Willie Devitt - a Gaelic games fanatic, as can be evidenced from the vast amount of memorabilia on the walls. In 2016 the pub was taken over by the Mangan brothers. As part of the tasteful makeover they introduced private whiskey lockers where the discerning drinker can leave their own bottle for safekeeping. Is 'bottle keep', as the Japanese and Americans call it, here to stay? Only time will tell. Devitt's is a well-established venue for Irish music and a popular venue for watching sports with no fewer than six high definition screens. It also has an impressively extensive selection of spirits. In the modern iteration of the Irish pub it is one that offers many things to many people.

Family Names and Irish Pubs

It became a legal requirement to display the proprietor's name over the front door of a pub in Ireland following the passage of legislation in 1872. Instigated by the authorities as a way of keeping tabs on drinking establishments for taxation purposes, the legacy of this law is often cited as one of the unique features of Irish pubs. Often a public house operates under a long-obsolete family name - a signature feature in the boom of 'Irish pubs' outside Ireland. This change in legislation limited the previous inventive array in names of Dublin pubs: the Sots Hole in Essex Street, the Wandering Jew in Castle Street, Three Candlesticks in King Street, House of Blazes in Aston Quay, the Blue Leg in High Street, the Holy Lamb in Cornmarket and the Golden Sugar Loaf in Abbey Street are all long since defunct. Some pubs, such as the Bleeding Horse and the Brazen Head, kept both a family name and original title.

13. Doheny and Nesbitt

5 Lower Baggot Street, Dublin 2, 01 6762945,
www.dohenyandnesbitts.ie

Doheny and Nesbitt is a pub of the old school: a stone floor, a couple of snugs, wooden partitions and dim lights. Ronan Foster described the pub in *In Dublin* magazine in 1976: 'There are a lot of people in this town who seem to be unable to enjoy a drink in anything other than uncomfortable surroundings; many of them can be found here. That said, it must also be said that this is a very pleasant pub indeed, even if it often proves difficult to raise your elbow above your waist.' The author recommended the snugs: 'These small enclosed rooms, each with access to the bar, are ideal for a quiet drink away from the bustling crowd outside. The trick is getting into one before someone else, and that is no mean feat.' Nothing much has changed in the interim.

These premises were first established as a pub in the 1840s under a lease held by William Burke, who ran it for over 50 years under the name Delahunty's. It passed through a number of hands before being bought and operated by Tipperary men Ned Doheny and Tom Nesbitt, who, after earning enough money in the United States, returned to Ireland in 1962 to put their names on it. It was sold on to current owners Tom and Paul Mannion in 1990.

It is with due reason the pub is sometimes referred to as the 'Doheny and Nesbitt School of Economics'. How it came to be the gathering point of political and economic opinion-shapers is a story told by John Waters in his book *Jiving at the Crossroads*, a memoir of the social, political and cultural landscape of Ireland in the 1980s. Niall Fleming worked in Madigan's bar in Donnybrook, beside RTE, the state television headquarters, where he became friendly with many influential employees, and obliged them by cashing cheques in the bar during a prolonged postal strike in the 1970s. When he left to work in a bar in Upper Baggot Street some of his RTE drinking friends followed him. They did not take to his new workplace, but soon discovered the pleasures of nearby Doheny and Nesbitt. It thus became the home of some influential people in Irish society. Waters listed the principle members of the 'school' in his book: Paul Tansey, the late economics correspondent with the *Irish Times*; Seán Barrett, a lecturer in economics at Trinity College; and the 'Dean', Colm McCarthy, who had worked for the Central Bank and the Economic, Social and Research Institute (ESRI). Journalists, high-ranking civil servants, members of the legal profession, and certain politicians also frequented the establishment. Vincent Browne, then editor of *Magill* magazine, provided a link to the media for the voices emerging from this unique locale. The group viewed Ireland as an economic basketcase and Browne eventually got tired listening to them, as he told Waters:

On the whole and in many cases individually, they are a terrible pain in the ass. They think they have the answer to everything. They also think they are very funny ... they are tickled to death by meeting people they otherwise deride – they get so chuffed if Charlie [the then leader of the government, Charles Haughey] speaks to them. They rush around to Doheny's to tell the others all about it, and what brilliant witticisms they said back there ... pathetic really .... They also love to go on television and they will tell you again and again how clever and witty they were and how foolish they made others look and all that ... none of these fellows give a bugger about anyone who is poor.

Dick Walsh, former political editor of the *Irish Times*, coined the acronym DANSE to describe the tenor of conversation popular in the pub. The Doheny and Nesbitt School of Economics was populated, inevitably, by Lords of the DANSE.

The pub has changed since John Waters wrote *Jiving at the Crossroads*. The original front bar is still the same, but a massive extension had been added on to the back. The pub's website is not shy in proclaiming the hostelry's charms:

Probably the most photographed pub in Dublin, Doheny & Nesbitt is considered an institution for convivial gatherings, a sanctuary in which to escape the ravages of modern life, and a shrine to everything that is admirable in a public house. If Ireland invented the pub, then Dublin's finest showpiece is that of Doheny & Nesbitt. The pub's carved timber, aged wooden floors and ornate papier-mâché ceiling, recently restored, are universally admired.

Doheny and Nesbitt is still frequented by the great and the good. However, the drinking habits of the chattering classes – and mostly everyone else in Ireland – have changed substantially since the 1980s. Drink-driving legislation and the trend towards home drinking are only two of the complex factors which have changed the weekday atmosphere of pubs such as Doheny and Nesbitt. Now it is equally the preserve of tourists in an area where some of the best pubs in the city and country are to be found. Doheny and Nesbitt is part of the Baggot Street Mile, arguably the best-known pub crawl in the country, and worth including on any itinerary of pubs in the capital city. You never know who you might bump into.

The Victorian Pub

The much-eulogised Victorian pubs of Dublin were an impor-
tation from Great Britain. The Victorian era – the period of
time during which Queen Victoria reigned – began on 20 June
1837 and ended with her death on 22 January 1901, and was
characterised by rapid industrial, economic and social development. During this time standards of living rose significantly for
many, and this was reflected in the vastly improved standards of
accommodation and public buildings, including public houses.
People expected higher standards than previously pertained,
and with the increased availability of disposable income it was
worth the investment for publicans. The Licensed Grocers' and
Vintners' Association (precursor of the current-day Licensed
Vintners' Association) sent delegations to Britain in the 1870s
to weigh up developments. They were duly impressed with what
they saw and the Victorian pub era began in Ireland.

The Dublin Victorian pub was various in its physical pres-
entation but generally included a grocery and was a significant
step above the beer houses and spirit grocers that had proliferated throughout the city before that point. The central concern
of these establishments was the installation of a high enough
standard of decor to attract genteel Victorian patrons. Some
were built from scratch while others were makeovers of existing
premises. The Victorian pub varied from the simple to the elaborate, but were characterised by a preponderance of polished
hardwoods, mirrors and brass fittings. The remaining Victorian
pubs in Dublin, as highlighted in this book, demonstrate the
variety of architectural and design detail: the pub fan can appreciate the convex and concave mirrors, stained glass partitions,
granite and hardwood bar tops, vaulted ceilings, oak floors,
elaborate carvings, snugs and – above all else – clocks that are
to be found throughout the city. The Victorian establishments
represent the golden age of the public house and are a significant component of the rich architectural and cultural heritage of
Dublin city. We are lucky to have those that are remaining, given
the mass desecration of similar establishments in times past.

14. The Duke

8-9 Duke Street, Dublin 2, 01 6799553, www.thedukedublin.com

Opened in 1822, the Duke became one of the city's busiest pubs when Charles Bianconi opened his coach travel business across the road, taking travellers to every big town in Ireland south of Carlow. Initially trading as the National Hotel and Tavern, it was a popular haunt of bagatelle and billiard players awaiting transport. The winners were awarded tokens which were exchangeable for drink. The Duke had a very distinct tavern token (or 'scrip') with shamrocks on an inner circle.

Duke Street was named after the Second Duke of Grafton, Charles FitzRoy (1683–1757), who was the Viceroy and Lord Lieutenant of Ireland from 1720 to 1724 and held extensive property interests in the area. The Duke claims to have the second oldest publican's licence in this part of the city. When pubs were at their greatest numbers

there were seven on this street alone. The first owner, Thomas Carroll, was a good friend of William Fitzpatrick, who owned Davy Byrne's just across the street, and both were instrumental in the formation of the Licensed Vintners' Association. It was when the Kennedy brothers – John and Patrick – bought the pub in 1886 that it came into its full flowering as it is today. They installed the elaborate Victorian frontage and brought the pub upmarket to make it a suitable drinking establishment for the well-heeled who ate in oyster taverns, for which the street had acquired a reputation, and the shoppers of nearby Grafton Street, then very much on the ascent as the retail area of choice for the more affluent citizenry. The pub changed hands a few more times before being purchased by current owner Tom Gilligan, the twelfth landlord of these historic premises in the heart of Dublin city, in 1988. Over the years Gilligan has extended the pub and developed an extensive new section upstairs, a popular location for parties.

The Duke has a long association with Home Rule and republican politics. Followers of Charles Stewart Parnell met here when it was under the stewardship of the Kennedy bothers. From the early twentieth century it became a popular meeting place for writers and political activists, and numbered James Joyce, James Stephens, Oliver St John Gogarty and Arthur Griffith among its former guests. It was also a haunt of Michael Collins, leader of the Irish War of Independence, who occasionally used the snug to plan terrorist activities. Before his death he was engaged to Kitty Kiernan, a niece of the then owner of the next-door Dive Oyster Bar.

In the 1940s and 1950s it was frequented by poet Patrick Kavanagh, his arch-enemy, writer Brendan Behan, and Flann O'Brian. Those of a literary bent may wish to seek out the framed letters written by James Joyce, hanging upstairs in a hidden corner. In one, dispatched from Paris in 1926, the writer expressed his delight to the publisher Harriet Shaw Weaver that *Dubliners* had gone into an eighth print edition. In the missive he informed Weaver that he once threw the original manuscript of *Ulysses* into a fire in a fit of anger but that it was rescued by the 'family fire brigade'. In a letter to the writer T.S. Eliot, dated New Year's Day 1932, Joyce expressed regret over the death of his father and the fact that he never got back to Ireland to see him despite promising that he would.

During the 1970s the pub was a popular hangout for those associated with the rock music scene in the capital, and numbered Paul Hewson – later to become Bono of U2 fame – among its regulars. It is now the launching point for the highly regarded Dublin Literary Pub Crawl.

Snugs

Snugs are a defining feature of many Irish pubs. Their name describes their character: small and separate, a place away from the rest of the pub. These self-contained units, usually at the top of a bar, were traditionally the preserve of women, who were not accepted, or did not feel comfortable, in the main bar. In his 1969 guide to Dublin pubs, Roy Bulson, calling himself 'Publin', wrote of the snug in Ryan's of Parkgate Street: 'The snug is in full working order, complete with latch mechanism to keep it to yourself and this is the place to deposit a lady, since the custom of the house does not readily admit of their presence elsewhere.' On the snug in Doheny and Nesbitt he noted that 'if you bring a lady both she, and the other drinkers, will probably be happier if you put her in the snug at the front, or in the back room, served through a hatch'. Snugs were also frequented by members of the clergy, police, important members of society, and occasional lovers. Additionally, snugs were places of business deals and matchmaking. Typically they had a wooden door with leaded glass above head height so the occupants could not be seen from outside. The seating was usually basic, and was frequently little more than wooden benches. In some of the more salubrious establishments (like Ryan's of Parkgate Street) the top section of the door was mirrored to further ensure privacy. In many cases snugs could be locked from the inside to ensure there were no unwelcome intruders. There was normally a bell to get the attention of the barman, and a hatch through which the drink was served. Over time they became a normalised part of the pub and were frequented by a mixed clientele. In parts of Britain it was common for the prices to be higher in the snug than the rest of the pub, but this did not generally tend to be the case in Ireland. Many snugs were torn out of bars during the lounge bar revolution of the 1960s and 1970s but, thankfully, there are some great ones remaining, particularly in the Victorian pubs in Dublin: Toner's, Doheny and Nesbitt, and Searson's are all on Baggot Street on the affluent south side, while the Palace and Ryan's, amongst others, fly the flag for the north side. Kehoe's on South Anne Street has another beautiful example.

15. Farrier and Draper

Powerscourt Townhouse, 59 South William Street, Dublin 2, 01 6771220, www.farrieranddraper.ie

If the visitor is after gentility, then this opulent establishment opened by the Mercantile Group in 2016 in one of Dublin's most impressive Georgian townhouses, may fit the bill. It consists of two impressive spaces: the Georgian Room and the Gallery. The former, with its plush armchairs, offers food during the day and a remarkable selection of alcohol. The Gallery, containing a remarkable array of art covering virtually every inch of its navy walls, high ceiling, and massive fireplace, should appeal to the discerning patron. Waiters and bar staffs are dressed in full 1920s garb, complete with Peaky Blinders hats, shirts and sleeve garters.

According to the PR the name of the emporium connects the contemporary and historical roles that South William Street and Powerscourt Townhouse played in the life of the city centre, as farriers and drapers plied their trade there in the eighteenth century. Powerscourt was once home to Richard Wingfield, 3rd Viscount Powerscourt (1730–1788), and his wife, Lady Amelia, who bought the townhouse to entertain guests during Parliament season. They also owned the beautiful Powerscourt Estate in Enniskerry, County Wicklow. Powerscourt House was designed by Robert Mack and is considered the third finest Georgian house in Dublin, behind Leinster House and Charlemont House respectively.

The hallway and landing were decorated in rococo style while the ceiling in the music room (now the Town Bride) and ballroom (now the Powerscourt Gallery), both designed by Michael Stapleton, are in the neo-classical style. Richard, known as the 'French Earl' because of his penchant for the latest Parisian fashions, died in the house in 1788 and was laid out in state for two days. After the abolition of the Irish Parliament the government brought the property for £15,000 in 1807 – £500 less than it cost to build it – and established the Stamp Office here, designed by Francis Johnston, architect of the GPO and Saint George's Church. It was later occupied by silk merchants Ferrier and Pollack. In 1981 it opened as a shopping centre.

16. The Ferryman

35 Sir John Rogerson's Quay, Grand Canal Dock, Dublin 2,
01 6717053, www.theferrymantownhouse.ie

Tom and Bernadette O'Brien bought the Ferryman in 1991 when this part of the city was a world removed from the land of corporate headquarters and high-end apartments that it is today. In those dark economic days this bar was nothing more than a single room. After a makeover in 1998, in which they incorporated the building on the corner of Cardiff Lane, the pub was reincarnated as a hotel, and continued its tradition of Irish music, helped in no small way by the musical abilities of the owners. The two buildings occupied by the Ferryman date to 1790, when they were built by Lord Cardiff. In the past, a ferry crossed the Liffey at this point, transporting workers from north to south of the river to work in the Gasometer, the Banana Factory, and Dublin's ship-building yard. As recently as the mid-1980s, Guinness boats carrying barrels of their famous brew sailed past.

This area of Dublin city has fundamentally changed and is now largely the preserve of prosperous urbanites, many of whom work in the greater Docklands area. It was the development of Grand Canal Dock which transformed this previously neglected part of the capital city. The major infrastructural project developed the derelict and contaminated 10-hectare gas site at the east end of Pearse Street into the hugely successful 250,000-square-metre Grand Canal Dock development, consisting of 80,000 square metres of offices, 1,200 apartments, 10,000 square metres of retail space, a 2,200 seat theatre, and a 150-bedroom five-star hotel. Silicon Docks, as the area is often referred to, is now home to the European headquarters of Google, Facebook, LinkedIn, and many more businesses of the brave new world of the twenty-first century.

Inevitably, this development and gentrification has diversified the clientele of the Ferryman. Where once white-collar workers were a rare sighting, they now flock here for after-work drinks, in what can sometimes be a frenetic atmosphere with more than a whiff of young urban prosperity and all that goes with it. Despite the rapidly changing demographics the bar has stuck to its core formula of great traditional fare and music. It is well worth the brisk walk from the city centre to sample the wares on offer in this real Dublin pub. It is also only a stone's throw away from the 3Arena (formerly known as the Point Depot), home to many of the biggest music concerts in Ireland, and a perfect place for a pre- or post-gig libation.

One that Got Away: The Irish House Pub

Critics sometimes point to the lack of vernacular architecture in Dublin pubs. Why do they all look the same as those in Great Britain? The truth is that the great Victorian pub was a British invention and those in Dublin were largely copied from examples in London and other British cities. There was one exceptional diamond in the rough though and for almost a century it was one of the most celebrated pubs in Dublin. Its striking exterior boasted six miniature monastic round towers jutting into the sky, and its ornate façade had elaborate stucco work featuring such home-grown heroes as Daniel O'Connell and Henry Grattan. It was O'Meara's – but better known as the Irish House – and it stood on the corner of Winetavern Street and Wood Quay in the heart of Dublin between 1870 and 1968. The building was inspired by the ideology underpinning the Celtic Renaissance of the latter part of the nineteenth century, an era when the forces of cultural nationalism were growing apace and were reflected in a flowering of literature and art harping back to the Celtic origins of Irish society. The new movement saw little manifestation in architecture expression, which made the Irish House all the more special. Built in 1870 by P.P. Kelly, the decorated façade included Celtic revival and nationalist subjects by stuccodores Burnet and Comerford. (Stucco is a type of cement and render made of limestone, plaster and sand; there are numerous examples of this work on many Dublin building exteriors.)

As well as the life-size figures of Daniel O'Connell and Henry Grattan addressing members of the Irish Parliament, the façade included a representation of Erin weeping over a string-less harp and six Irish wolfhounds. While popular with the public, it was less so with the architectural press. The *Irish Builder* in June 1870 wrote thus: 'The genius who designed the unsightly structure now in process of erection at the corner of Winetavern Street on the quays (which we understand is intended as a gin palace), having no scope in the sub-structure, directed his entire attention to the super. We were for a considerable time puzzled to discover what its skyline was intended to represent, but plasterers have been busily engaged up it for the past few weeks, and they have brought into view, by plentiful applica-tion of Portland cement, six ludicrous imitations of round towers perched upon its parapet.' (The Irish House building was famously used as a backdrop for Joe Strick's film adaption of *Ulysses* in 1965. While Joyce's Leopold Bloom had his snack at Davy Byrne's on Duke Street, Strick moved the scene to the Irish House, where Milo O'Shea played Bloom. Racist taunts aimed at Bloom from midday drinkers resulted in a scene outside the pub.)

The Irish House was demolished in the late 1960s to make way for the controversial Dublin Corporation offices. Today it is no more than a memory to an older generation of Dubliners. Parts of the façade are said to be in possession of members of Dublin Civic Trust. At one stage there were plans to install it in the Guinness Storehouse but the idea came to naught. It is a terrible pity that it has not survived.

17. The George

89 South Great George's Street, Dublin 2, 01 4782983,
www.thegeorge.ie

The George is Dublin's best-known gay pub, and is an important part of the development of modern Ireland, a country that came late to the recognition of gay rights – a legacy of a country heavily dominated by the powers of the Catholic Church for so long. Opened in 1985 by Cyril O'Brien, eight years before homosexuality was decriminal-ised in Ireland, the George now has more competition, but it is still a central part of the gay scene in Dublin. When it opened the only other gay venue in the city was the Viking on Dame Street, although Bartley Dunne's and Rice's on Saint Stephen's Green had long been unofficial meeting places for those who did not feel they belonged in the straitjacketed code of sexuality promulgated by the overweening Catholic Church. All three are now sadly gone.

The George takes its name from its location; in medieval times this was the site of the Church of Saint George. Records show that the first commercially licenced premises here was a shellfish tavern dating back to 1780, and that families called Quelchs, Keshans, Ryans and O'Dwyers were all one-time publicans here.

The lavender-painted exterior was a clarion cry for a more inclusive and mature Ireland and soon become a much-loved part of Dublin's street furniture. The oldest and smallest bar in the complex is jokingly referred to as 'Jurassic Park' because of its popularity with older clients, while the front bar is known as Bridie's, in honour of a long-serving member of staff, now deceased.

When O'Brien first opened the George he transformed the upstairs into a gay disco called the Loft, complete with Tivoli lighting, which some wags rather harshly described as being like the inside of a hairdresser's brain. It further expanded in 1998 when he purchased an adjacent building, which had formerly housed an Indian restaurant. Newer gay venues in the city include the Front Lounge on Parliament Street and Pantibar on Capel Street – the latter owned by Rory O'Neill, AKA Panti Bliss – but the venerable George still manages to keep its place in the fabric of twenty-first-century gay life in Dublin. It is particularly well known for its long-running drag show, and is synonymous with gay cultural icon Shirley Temple Bar – AKA Declan Buckley – who has been running a hugely popular bingo night here since 1997.

The pub made the news in June 2008, on the eve of the Dublin Gay Pride Festival, when a hoax caller announced that he had planted a bomb on the premises. To the annoyance of many, the police had to evacuate the premises at 11 p.m., but the celebrations were reignited ninety minutes later when the owners were given the all-clear. The party has continued ever since. In 2015 the establishment was acquired by the Mercantile Group. In May 2017 homophobic graffiti appeared on the outside of the premises but, as they have done before, the owners shrugged their shoulders in the face of this ignorance, and got on with the business of providing first-class entertainment to its many patrons, both gay and straight.

18. The Gravity Bar at the Guinness Storehouse

Saint James's Gate, Dublin 8, 01 4084800,
www.guinnessstorehouse.com

The Gravity Bar is different to every other drinking emporium in this guide: you have to pay to get in. This unique venue is on the seventh floor of the Guinness Storehouse, and is the final part of the tour of Ireland's most visited tourist attraction. After taking in the delights of the Guinness story the visitor can finish here with – what has no excuse for not being – 'the best pint of Guinness in Dublin'. The bar has a 360-degree panoramic view of the city and is open to the general public outside of the Guinness Experience opening hours, as well as for corporate bookings. The Guinness Storehouse has proven a remarkable success story. In 2016, 1,647,408 people visited 'the home of the black stuff', as the marketing literature has it, a full 10 per cent increase on the previous year.

The building in which the Storehouse is located was constructed in 1902 as a fermentation plant for the Saint James's Gate Brewery. Designed in the style of the Chicago School of Architecture, it was the first multi-storey steel-framed building in Ireland. The operation was decommissioned in 1988 when a new fermentation plant opened nearby. The Guinness Storehouse opened for business as a tourist attraction in 2000, with a further wing opened in 2006. In May 2011, Queen Elizabeth II and Prince Philip visited the Storehouse as part of a state visit to Ireland, a sure indication of its centrality to Irish social and cultural history. There is a plethora of activities to occupy the visitor. The 9,000-year lease signed by Arthur Guinness on the brewery site is on display on the bottom floor, while visitors may pour their own pint of Guinness in the Perfect Pint Bar. The Brewery Bar on the fifth floor offers Irish cuisine, using Guinness both in the cooking and as an accompaniment to food. The third and fourth floors of the Storehouse are home to the Arthur Guinness Business Centre, an area with training and conference facilities. The extensive Guinness Archive is also based at the Storehouse and contains photographs, film, memorabilia, posters, maps, bottles and artefacts documenting the history of the Guinness company, brand and products. A drink in the Gravity Bar is a well-deserved treat for the visitor who has taken the extensive body of information on board.

19. Grogan's/Castle Lounge

15 William Street South, Dublin 2, 01 6779320, www.facebook.com/ groganscastlelounge/

Grogan's is widely regarded as the last outpost of what remains of 'Bohemian Dublin', and its unique environment has a remarkable appeal across various demographic groups; Grogan's is many things to many people, and, as well as an interesting and diverse clientele, the pub has had a colourful past in its own right. From the 1840s until 1885 Anne Ledwidge owned a butcher shop here, and was the official meat supplier to the city's most important resident, the Lord Lieutenant of Dublin. In 1885 the building was turned into a spirit grocer, which was run successively by James Moran, James Bowe (a member of the family that owned Bowe's on Fleet Street), Michael Finnegan and Tommy Smith. In 1948 the name was changed to the Castle Bar Wine and Spirit Merchant, while J. Grogan's name was added in 1959.

There are solid reasons as to why the pub is so well-supported by the artistic and literary communities of the city. The walls of the bar are covered with the work of local artists, all of which can be bought and brought home at the end of the night. Twice a year the walls are cleared to make room for new pieces and, laudably, no commission is taken by the pub on any sales. The pub makes further contributions to the artistic and literary community by holding book and poetry launches on a regular basis.

When McDaid's pub, the former headquarters of the mid-century literary scene in Dublin, went up for sale the renowned head barman Paddy O'Brien tried to buy it, but was outbid by 'an English woman who wanted to own a literary pub in Dublin'. O'Brien, invited by his friend Tommy Smith who bought it on the same day he failed to acquire McDaid's, moved to Grogan's in 1972 and brought many of his artistic clientele with him, although many of the leading lights of the 1950s generation had died out by then – ravaged, in many cases, by the effects of alcoholism.

The decor of Grogan's can best be described as shabby, and the crowd cross-generational and eclectic. It is particularly and fondly well-known for its toasted sandwiches and package soup – a far cry from the many restaurants and gastropubs in the immediate upmarket locality. There is no better quintessential Dublin experience than whiling away a couple of hours here with a few pints of Guinness – and a toasted sandwich if needed – watching the world pass by, either from the inside or at one of the tables outside on the heated patio which wraps around the entire building.

In 1993 the owners commissioned stained glass artist Katherine Lamb to capture a cross-section of the pub's customers. The resultant 'The Day People' and 'The Night People' are two pieces of art that are definitely not for sale. The former is a standard stained glass piece and includes depictions of the now deceased actor Donal McCann and the owner among a large group of customers of the time, while the latter is a screen painting of a gregarious group of night-time drinkers.

That Grogan's can be considered a local pub is a feat in itself. Despite being situated in the heart of Dublin's shopping, entertainment and culinary centre, it has a loyal core group of dedicated attendees. There is no television and no recorded or live music in Grogan's – an increasing rarity in these frenetic and market-driven times. It is a pub that has become great by not changing at all. The decor is decidedly 1970s, identical to the lounges which were added to bars all over the country mostly in an effort to feminise the premises in the era of the 'Lounge Bar'. The navy floral carpet has definitely seen better days, and the terracotta tiles on the floor of the small bar at the back are not in keeping with newer pubs, older pubs, or those made to look old. The rudimentary white roof tiles and the old air conditioning units are certainly an indication of the preference for functionality over any aesthetic consideration in this unique pub; it really is like nowhere else in Dublin.

Inevitably, Grogan's also has strong literary links. It features in Flann O'Brien's novel *At Swim Two Birds* in an episode where the narrator goes to the pub with a young failed medical student by the name of Kelly: 'We sat in Grogan's with our faded overcoats finely disarrayed on easy chairs in the mullioned snug. I gave a penny and two shillings to a civil man who brought us in return two glasses of black porter, imperial pint measure. I adjusted the glasses to the front of each of us and reflected on the solemnity of the occasion. It was my first taste of porter.' The pub goes on to feature a number of times in the narrative as a bolthole for the main protagonist, who is not afraid to mention his purpose: 'That same afternoon I was sitting on a barstool in an intoxicated condition in Grogan's licensed premises.' O'Brien himself was not averse to whiling away his own afternoons in Grogan's and many other hostelries around the city.

In a 2011 interview, owner Tommy Smith outlined his philosophy to Una Mullally of the *Irish Times*: 'It doesn't make a difference where you come from here, that's what we like. I'd like to think that this pub is quite egalitarian. There's no such thing as suits or just younger people or just old people. It's just people who want to talk to each other. We don't have televisions or background music. Not everyone wants to go out and boogey all the time, some people want to meet up and talk about something more serious. I think this pub is a place where you can do that; from legal age to whatever age you live to. People can mingle here.'

It is hard to argue with Smith's thesis as the basis for a perfect pub. Grogan's continues to be a unique presence in Dublin pub culture.

The Lounge Bar Revolution

Under the severe eye of the Catholic Church the Irish pub has historically been a male-dominated space, and it was not until the 1960s that women started to be made more widely welcome. Accounts of pubs in the nineteenth century point to a greater number of women being present than is often thought, and it was the overweening power appropriated by the Church after the Great Famine of 1845–1849 that clamped down on public enjoyment and reinforced the role of the woman as homemaker only. With the changing mores of the 1960s publicans realised the often Spartan furnishings of the public bar were an insufficient attraction to the female customer, and many built on lounges complete with carpets and soft furnishings. These additional spaces were akin to bringing the comforts of the home into the drinking establishment. Lounge bars were frequently built with an eye to musical performance, and sometimes incorporated stages and sound systems. Travelling the length and breadth of Ireland, 'Lounge Bar' signs are everywhere apparent. Not all were installed in sympathy with existing buildings and the lounge bar revolution sometimes went hand-in-hand with the demise of many fine historical pubs, particularly in cities. As fashions evolve recent times have seen many lounge bars recon-figured and the banquettes which typified the era are becoming rarer, swallowed up in a further outbreak of faux-Victoriana or the latest postmodern trends. The evolution of Irish pubs continues apace.

20. Hartigan's

100 Lower Leeson Street, Dublin 2, 01 676 2280,
www.facebook.com/pages/Hartigans/103208446411831

There is no other pub quite like Hartigan's in Dublin city. It could variously be described as a country bar in the city or a dive bar in want of a little tender love and care. With its frayed linoleum tiles, off-canary yellow paint, and rudimentary beer garden, it can almost feel like being in a down-at-heel sports dressing room, but therein lies the charm. In a city where each new bar attempts to have a more unique concept than the previous one, this establishment is a throwback, and a slice of old Dublin at its best. If the visitor really wants to see how the Irish pub has evolved over time this one is a must. Hartigan's has long been a home from home for one of the most eclectic clienteles in the city and has a genuine claim for the best pint of Guinness in the city, a sworn fact by many fans of this charming pub. It is a place where many people feel comfortable in a world of increasingly rarefied drinking experiences. From 1974 it has been owned by the Mulligans, who brought up eight children over the premises. The late and much lamented Alfie Mulligan died in 2012 at the age of 90. His wife, Evelyn 'Ma' Mulligan, has kept the premises going since. The story of their acquisition of the pub is an often repeated one. Alfie came from a farm in Leitrim, was educated in Cork and served his apprenticeship as a barman in Glasgow before returning to Ireland where he managed Mooney's pub in Phibsboro. One day he suffered a burst ulcer and found himself in Saint Vincent's Hospital, then on Saint Stephen's Green. Wanting to tell his wife Evelyn where he was, he found a payphone in a public house on Leeson Street. He owned it within a year.

The pub featured in Flann O'Brien's surrealist novel *At Swim Two Birds* and has long been a haunt of University College Dublin (UCD) students, and even boasts a past pupil's union called Sotrah – derived by spelling Harto's (a commonly used shortened form of the pub's name) backwards.

If Hartigan's is good enough for multi-millionaire entrepreneur Denis O'Brien then it should serve most others' needs. For his fiftieth birthday the communications mogul celebrated in style by constructing a marquee replica of the bar in the grounds of Wanderers' Rugby Football Club, as the original was not able to cope with all 700 guests. That is flattery.

21. The Horseshoe Bar in the Shelbourne Hotel

27 Saint Stephen's Green, Dublin 2, 01 6634500,
www.shelbournedining.ie

If the walls of the Horseshoe Bar could speak, they could provide a comprehensive account of modern Irish social and cultural history as it was viewed by the chattering classes and well-heeled patrons who have long frequented this urbane premises since its opening on 26 November 1957. From Brendan Behan to Princess Grace of Monaco, Bill Clinton to Julia Roberts and Liam Neeson, this bar has entertained the great and the good. The now deceased P.J. Mara, spin doctor for the late and controversial former Taoiseach Charles Haughey, even held his eagerly awaited press conferences here on Friday afternoons while 'The Boss', as Haughey was widely known, was in power.

The name of the bar derives from the shape of the counter, although, given its long association with the hunting set, this may not be the total truth. It was listed as one of the 'Top 100 Bars' in the world by *Newsweek International* magazine in 1985, and with its marble top bar, shining brass artefacts and deep red walls it is not hard to see why. It was designed by Sam Stephenson, Ireland's answer to a 'starchitect' of that time, whose Brutalism-inspired work has engendered heated debate over the years. Stephenson also designed the Central Bank of Ireland on Dame Street (1975), the ESB Headquarters at Fitzwilliam Street (1976) and the Dublin Corporation Offices at Woodquay (1976), all controversial edifices in their day.

If the environment of the Horseshoe Bar is too rarefied, there is a second pub on the hotel premises called the No. 27 Bar and Lounge. When finished with an aperitif the diner can make their short way into the Saddle Room, one of Dublin's most elite gastronomic experiences. There is also the Lord Mayor's Lounge where it is traditional to take afternoon tea.

The Shelbourne Hotel was established in 1824 by Tipperary man Martin Burke, who expressed a wish to 'woo genteel custom who wanted solid, comfortable and serviceable accommodation at a fashionable address'. The building had originally been the townhouse of Thomas Fitzgerald, the First Earl of Kerry, and later served as an army billet before being burned down in 1818. Burke named it after William Petty, Second Earl of Shelburne and Prime Minister of Great Britain from July 1782 to April 1783. It soon established a reputation as a suitable location for the Anglo-Irish 'quality' on their visits to the city from their country mansions and estates. The Shelbourne was the first hotel in Ireland to be lit by gaslight, and, complete with a ladies' coffee room, smoking room, hairdressing salon, reading room and telegraph office, soon became a popular locale for those involved with the creative arts. George Moore was inspired to write *A Drama in Muslin* during a stay here while Graham Greene wrote part of *The End of the Affair* while in residence. Like all good old hotels worth their salt, the Shelbourne is reportedly haunted, in this case by the ghost of Mary Masters, a young girl who lived in the area who died of cholera when she was only seven years old, in 1846. Despite numerous attempts to remove her ghostly presence she has frequently been seen by staff and guests over the years, and annoyingly causes curtains to billow at 27 Saint Stephen's Green.

The Shelbourne has witnessed many historic episodes. The constitution of the Irish Free State was drafted in Room 112 in May 1922 under the leadership of Michael Collins; the Irish traditional music group The Chieftains was formed in the bar; and Irish actor Peter O'Toole once took a bath in champagne during a stay. James Cagney once danced on the piano; John F. Kennedy paid a visit here in 1958; and, perhaps most infamously of all, Alois Hitler, a half-brother of the German dictator, worked here as a wine waiter before World War I. He later married Irish woman Bridget Dowling after they eloped to London. Alois introduced Bridget to his brother in Liverpool and then abandoned her.

The Shelbourne is Dublin's largest five-star hotel and was given a comprehensive makeover in 2007 and again in early 2019, bringing the luxury quotient to a new level. The 'Old Lady of Stephen's Green', as this salubrious establishment is sometimes called, now has 265 bedrooms. If an expensive drink in rarefied surroundings is required it would be hard to bypass the Horseshoe Bar in the Shelbourne Hotel.

Irish Coffee

The story of the invention of the iconic alcoholic drink Irish coffee – a mixture of hot coffee, Irish whiskey, sugar and unwhipped cream – is an interesting one. It was reputedly invented by Joe Sheridan in Foynes, County Limerick (an airport at that time), in the 1940s when he provided it to a group of American tourists on a cold winter evening. The story goes that it was subsequently brought to San Francisco in 1952 by travel writer Stanton Delaplane after he tasted it at nearby Shannon Airport. The classical recipe is simple. Black coffee is poured into the mug, after which whiskey and at least one level teaspoon of sugar – preferably brown – is stirred in, until fully dissolved. The sugar is essential for floating liquid cream on top. Thick cream is carefully poured over the back of a spoon, initially held just above the surface of the coffee, and then gradually raised a little. The layer of cream will float on the coffee without mixing. The coffee is then drunk through the layer of cream. What could be more Irish than that?

22. The International Bar

23 Wicklow Street, Dublin 2, 01 6779250, www.international-bar.com

For many people the International Bar on Wicklow Street is synonymous with its famous Comedy Cellar (located upstairs), established in 1988, which gave comedians like Ardal O'Hanlon of *Father Ted*

fame, Tommy Tiernan, Des Bishop and Dara Ó Briain, amongst others, their first start in the business. Budding talents can still try their hand on Wednesday nights.

The International is about much more than comedy though; it is a fine example of the history and beauty to be seen in the finest of Dublin pubs. After entering the impressive premises the patron's eye is immediately drawn to the one-piece reredos – more often seen to the rear of church altars – behind the polished pink granite bar, on which are carved seven wooden figureheads representing the seven river gods of Ireland. These ornamental screens are a rarity, and the lucky customer can justifiably claim to be expanding his artistic knowledge while imbibing a drink of choice and resting his feet on the beautiful brass foot rails around the bar, another feature of many public houses designed in the high Victorian style.

John Dunne became the first registered owner of the premises in 1854, continuing to run it until selling it on to the O'Donoghue family in 1886. It has stayed in the O'Donoghue family ever since; the family motto is visible on the ground inside the main door.

In *Ulysses* James Joyce refers to the pub by the common appellation of the time, 'Ruggy O'Donoghue's', when he is describing a shopping expedition of 'Master Dignam', son of Paddy Dignam, whose funeral takes place on the day the book is set: 'Opposite Ruggy O'Donohue's Master Patrick Aloysius Dignam pawing the pound and a half of Mangan's, late Fehrenbacks, porksteaks he had been sent for went along warm Wicklow Street dawdling.'

The International is also associated with the Spanish Civil War, as the Irish Socialist Brigade held regular meetings here before 200 of them departed for Spain under the command of Frank Ryan. Ryan opposed the fascism of the Blueshirts in Ireland, and that of Franco in Spain. With the courage of his convictions he led the 'Connolly Column', alongside the myriad other members of the International Brigade, to defend the democratic and socialist Second Spanish Republic against Franco's Nationalists. The name of the pub turned out to be highly appropriate: the 'Internationale' has long been the song which calls socialists to arms the world over. Ryan was seriously injured, arrested and condemned to death, although his sentence was later commuted to life in prison. After being handed over to German authorities by the Spanish he was brought back to Ireland in a German submarine. Ryan later returned to Berlin, where he died unexpectedly from an illness that he most likely acquired while in prison in Burgos in Spain.

The International Bar also claims a small part in the folk and ballad boom in Ireland of the 1960s and 1970s. Luke Kelly met Ronnie Drew in the bar, after the former had returned from working in the United Kingdom, and shortly afterwards they went on to form the Dubliners, the most famous and enduring of all the folk groups to emerge from the period.

These days the pub is always busy, and is popular with tourists and natives alike. There is comedy seven nights a week in the upstairs bar, while the ground floor has frequent traditional Irish music sessions. During the week the basement section of this three-storey premises houses jazz performers, poetry, and singer-songwriter nights. This is a pub that has something for everyone.

23. Jimmy Rabbitte's

84-87 Lower Camden Street, Dublin 2, 01 5367300,
www.facebook.com/jimmyrabbittes

This trendy pub is named after a character from the 1987 Roddy Doyle novel *The Commitments*, which tells the story of a group of unemployed Dublin musicians and their attempts to establish a soul band. The book was subsequently made into a hugely successful film of the same name by British director Alan Parker, and, if the pub proves as successful as either of those, it will be a surefire winner.

Jimmy Rabbitte's is owned by the same team who run the Palace on Camden Street (once Ricardo's Snooker Hall and, fittingly, a location used during the filming of *The Commitments*), the Living Room, and the Czech Inn. There are some unusual design features in this establishment, including portraits of animals wearing human clothes and pseudo-antique landscapes complete with UFOs on the walls. The pub's outdoor area is decorated with street art and features beautiful dark wood benches. At the time of writing the backyard features a newly installed Pitt Brothers pop-up operating out of a converted shipping container serving barbecued food. Of the many new ventures in the city in the last five years shrewd observers reckon this could be a stayer. Only time will tell.

24. John Fallon's (The Capstan Bar)

129 The Coombe, Dublin 8, 01 4542801
www.facebook.com/John-Fallons-The-Capstan-Bar-112050775539357

Also known as the Capstan Bar – named after the British cigarettes of the same name, which were once very popular on the Irish market because they were the strongest available – there was a sharp intake of breath by many fans of this old-world premises when it changed hands and pulled down its shutters in early 2015. Thankfully, the closure was temporary and it reopened under the stewardship of Conor Linnane, who also owns the Dawson Lounge, the smallest bar in the city (and perhaps the country). Fallon's pub is located on the corner of Dean Street and New Street South, directly opposite Saint Patrick's Cathedral in the heart of Dublin's Liberties, an area of the city which holds a special place in the heart of many Dubliners. This historic locale, originally a valley where a tributary of the River Poddle called the Coombe Stream ran, is so called because it did not come under the jurisdiction of the city authorities due to its location outside the medieval city walls. It was an area originally populated by weavers and wool merchants, many of whom were emigrants from England, France and Holland. The French settlers were Huguenot refugees who had fled the persecutions of Louis XIV in the late seventeenth century, and they brought with them a strong Protestant work ethic. Some of the streets at the western end of the Coombe, like Chamber Street, Pool Street and Weaver Street, are still referred to as 'Huguenot Streets'. The prosperity engendered by the arrival of these economic migrants did not last, and at the end of eighteenth century the Liberties were described by a staff member of the Dublin Castle administrative headquarters as 'a scene of the most abject poverty, deplorable sickness and a magazine of fury'. Despite this endemic poverty the area has a long history of markets of all types, reflected in nearby street names, which include Fishamble Street, Winetavern Street, Cook Street and the Corn Market. While trade continued to a certain degree – the area of Thomas Street near Fallon's pub has long been associated with the antique trade – this part of Dublin was persistently neglected by the city authorities and saw a significant amount of urban decay and social problems over the course of the twentieth century. As the economy has improved and Dublin moves relentlessly forward the area is gradually coming to its feet again with extensive apartment building in recent years.

While there is a stone marker outside the pub with the year 1620 carved on it, there is no supporting evidence to suggest a pub stood here at that time. The extant premises date to 1911 after it was rebuilt following a fire. However, there is no doubt that the location had a different pub on the site before then, as it is known that Dan Donnelly, a famous nineteenth-century boxer, once ran a drinking establishment here. Donnelly, one of an impoverished family of seventeen from the Dublin Docks area, was the first Irish-born heavyweight boxing champion. After a hugely successful career he tried his hand as a publican and owned four Dublin pubs at different times. However, the famous sportsman was given to drink and general debauchery, and all of his business interests ultimately proved unprofitable. He died in 1820 at Donnelly's Public House, his last business concern – now Fallon's – at the tragically young age of 32. By a twisted pathway Dan Donnelly's arm has become part of Irish pub folklore. Following his death the boxer was buried at the nearby Bully's Acre cemetery, but a few nights later his body was robbed and brought to an eminent Dublin surgeon who paid for cadavers. Friends of Donnelly got wind of the story and went to the surgeon's residence, threatening to kill him if he did not return the body. After a quick negotiation the doctor agreed to return the body, as long as he could keep the right arm for medical purposes. The story goes that the arm was painted with red lead paint to preserve it, and then travelled onwards to a Scottish medical college where it was used by students for a number of years to study anatomy. It later became an exhibit in a Victorian travelling circus and was promoted as 'the longest arm in the history of pugilism'. In 1904 it was acquired by Belfast publican Hugh 'Texas' McAlevey, who displayed it in his pub for a number of years before storing it away in an attic. Through some unknown means it ended up in Kilcullen, County Kildare, in the 1950s, where publican Jim Byrne decided to use it as part of a recreation of a famous fight Donnelly had been involved in at the nearby Curragh camp, in which the Irishman had unexpectedly defeated heavyweight champion George Cooper. The successful re-enactment was part of An Tóstal, a nationwide Irish festival started at the time by the government in an effort to promote rural tourism. After the exhibition, the arm was put on display in the Hideout pub in Kilcullen (owned by the aforementioned Jim Byrne), where it remained for 43 years, until the publican died in 2006.

Amazingly, the arm was subsequently brought to the United States in the cockpit of an Aer Lingus jet to use as part of an exhibition called 'Fighting Irishmen: A Celebration of the Celtic Warrior', which toured across the nation. It returned to the Ulster Folk Park Museum in Omagh, County Tyrone, before eventually coming to rest in the Gaelic Athletic Association Museum in Croke Park in Dublin in 2010, where it has now found a permanent home.

The junction which Fallon's faces onto was once home to five pubs and went by the colourful name of the four corners of hell. The four corners were occupied by Kenny's, Quinn's, O'Beirne's and Lowe's, with Fallon's near at hand looking at all four pubs. With the widening of the junction in the 1980s Fallon's was the only premises left standing.

The atmosphere in this beautiful slice of old Dublin is enhanced by the stove, the heavy dark wood, and the beautiful snug. It may be one of the smaller pubs around, but it punches well above its weight, and is a welcome haven for locals and visitors alike. Long may it last.

Dublin's Smallest Pub: The Dawson Lounge

The Dawson Lounge is Dublin's smallest pub (and may also be the smallest pub in Ireland), with a capacity of just over forty. It is so small that there are cushions on the roof of the ladies' toilets. Located in the most affluent shopping area of the city, and cheek by jowl with some of the trendiest bars and restaurants in the capital, this is a unique watering hole. One of the best features is the proximity of the bar. No matter where you are in the room, service is only a few steps away, but if you suffer from claustrophobia it might be best avoided. The fact that it is underground compounds the sense of entrapment for those who do not like that sort of thing.

25. Kehoe's

9 South Anne Street, Dublin 2, 01 6778312,
www.louisfitzgerald.com/kehoes

First licensed in 1803, Kehoe's, with its beautiful mahogany features, quaint snugs and sloping floor, is among the most charming of the Victorian pubs left in Dublin. The Victoriana, like all the great examples in Dublin, dates from the last years of the nineteenth century. It could not be considered high Victorian in the way of the Long Hall or the Palace Bar, for example, but it is beautiful for what it is, characterised by small intimate spaces and mahogany wood panels dividing the space along the bar. It is intimate yet beautiful, a true work of art. After the streets around this part of the city were laid out by Joshua Dawson it became one of the most affluent and desirable areas to live in Dublin, and property here still commands the highest prices in the capital's centre. Kehoe's is in a great location with a particularly wonderful view of the nearby Saint Anne's Church.

Situated a mere stone's throw from Grafton Street, the premier shopping street in the capital city, Kehoe's is a window into the past once you enter through the swing door surrounded by beautiful antique mirrors. These details are a sharp counterpoint to the red and green neon sign outside which alerts passers-by to its seductive presence. Like so many older pubs in the city it was once a spirit grocer, and the original mahogany drawers (there are 28 of them), holding tea, snuff and other daily provisions, are still in evidence behind a low grocery counter to the left as you enter the premises from South Anne Street.

The beautiful snug comes complete with buzzer to command the attention of the bartender when service is required, although given the crowds that attend this hostelry, particularly at the weekend, it is not always easy to get an immediate response.

Under John Kehoe's stewardship in the mid-twentieth century the pub had a reputation for being conservative and tightly run. Patrick Kavanagh, Brendan Behan and Flann O'Brien all imbibed here, but their high jinks were always kept in order by the strict proprietor. It was a pub they attended in the morning before outright inebriation brought on regrettable behaviour. After Kavanagh fell out with the owner of McDaid's he became a more regular drinker in Kehoe's.

Unlike many of the other pubs in the vicinity, Kehoe's is nothing approaching a gastropub – unless the visitor considers ham and cheese toasted sandwiches haute cuisine. It is a simply laid-out establishment with a narrow bar at the front and a larger lounge at the back, known as 'The Heritage Bar', complete with two small ante rooms. The toilets are a low point – be sure to lower your head before entering them as they claim to have the lowest entry in all of Dublin.

When John Kehoe died the pub was bought by serial publican Louis Fitzgerald for over £2,000,000. Thankfully, he left the premises untouched, except to open the upstairs area and install a bar in the rooms where Kehoe had lived during his tenure. There is a distinct slope to the floor – so steep in fact, that it does not look safe to put a drink on the wooden dresser beside the fireplace, in case it might slide off the edge onto the ground. Upstairs, it is almost impossible to believe that the hustle and bustle of Grafton Street is nearby. This pub has a unique atmosphere that so many thousand others seek to obtain but rarely fail to achieve. In March 2017 the Licensed Vintners' Association celebrated their two hundredth anniversary with a spectacular evening in the nearby Mansion House. Fittingly, Kehoe's won the award for the best pub in Dublin, a ringing endorsement by the members of an exclusive club.

James Joyce and Dublin Pubs

'*Good puzzle would be cross Dublin without passing a pub.*'
James Joyce, *Ulysses*

Leopold Bloom, the main character in *Ulysses*, posed his famous puzzle as he went to buy a kidney for his breakfast on the morning of 16 June 1904. James Joyce had a wonderful Dublin pub pedigree. His father, John Stanislaus Joyce, brought penury on the family through his drinking exploits in the hostelries of the city, while his mother was the daughter of a publican in the Eagle House Tavern in Terenure (formerly Roundtown), on the southern edge of Dublin. Joyce once famously told his friend Frank Budgen, an English painter and writer, about his vision for *Ulysses*: 'I want to give a picture of Dublin so complete that if the city one day suddenly disappeared from the earth it could be reconstructed out of my book.' This he certainly did. Joyce had a vast knowledge of Dublin, but he also used a copy of *Thom's Directory* from 1904 when he was writing Ulysses. *Thom's Directories* classify Dublin since 1844, listing, amongst other things, businesses, street addresses, nobility and gentry in Dublin on an annual basis. In *Ulysses*, Joyce mentions over seventy places where alcohol was sold – almost equally split between the north side and south side of Dublin. Roughly half still exist.

Leopold Bloom is given to rumination on the most obscure topics through the course of the novel; one such fixation is pub economics and location. He considered the position of Doyle's (formerly Dunphy's) in Phibsboro: 'Dunphy's corner. Mourning coaches drawn up, drowning their grief. A pause by the wayside. Tiptop position for a pub. Expect we'll pull up here on the way back to drink his health. Pass round the consolation. Elixir of life.' The pub was close to Glasnevin cemetery – hence the patrons drowning their grief. It was, and is, a 'tiptop' location.

Bloom also evaluated the nearby Larry O'Rourke's, on Eccles Street, now the Eccles Townhouse: 'He approached Larry O'Rourke's. From the cellar grating floated up the flabby gush of porter. Through the open doorway the bar squirted out whiffs of ginger, tea dust, biscuitmush. Good house, however: just the end of the city traffic.' Leopold Bloom was not as impressed with the location of the Big Tree (formerly McAuley's): 'For instance McAuley's down there: n.g. as position. Of course if they ran a tramline along the North Circular from the cattlemarket to the quays value would go up like a shot.' Bloom must have been prescient – the Big Tree is soon to be demolished.

Joyce had arguments with his proposed publisher George Roberts about using the real names of pubs and publicans in his short story collection *Dubliners*. On 23 August 1912 he wrote to his brother Stanislaus to outline his defence to Roberts for naming the pubs, making the following points:

i.   Public houses are mentioned in four stories out of 15. In 3 of these stories the names are fictitious. In the 4th the names are real because the persons walk from place to place ('Counterparts')
ii. Nothing happens in the public houses. People drink.
iii. I offered to take a car and go with Roberts, proofs in hand, to the 3 or 4 publicans really named and to the secretary of the railway co. He refused.
iv. I said the publicans would be glad of the advertisement.
v.   I said that I would put in fictitious names for the few real ones but added that by so doing the selling value in Dublin of the book would go down.

In the end he did not get his way.

26. The Library Bar at the Central Hotel

1 Exchequer Street, Dublin 2, 01 6797302,
www.centralhoteldublin.com

The Library Bar in the three-star Central Hotel is a throwback to an old-world atmosphere, and provides a welcome break for the achingly hip world of contemporary Dublin social life. The now 70-bedroom hotel was built in 1887 by Ross and Walpole, and was designed by Richard Millar and William Symens of Kildare Street. The Library Bar is a haven of peace in a frantic part of the city: there is no music, understated table service, beautiful period furniture – including sumptuous couches (sofas) and armchair – a discreet snug and glowing fireplaces.

There is also an inevitable link to Michael Collins, who set up his first office in Dublin across the road at Number 10 Exchequer Street

when he returned home from Frongoch internment camp in Wales. Collins is reputed to have put up IRA men in the Central Hotel when they were in Dublin to visit him on official business. It is also said the British military used the hotel for accommodation, so there may have been a few interesting meetings in the corridors.

Despite the air of studied antiquity, the wonder of it all is that the Library Bar only dates from 1991, when the hotel reopened under new ownership. As part of a redesign the owners converted space previously used as offices into the current format. The essence of the Library Bar is a simple but difficult achievement: it is a destination bar in a hotel. There is nothing else quite like it in Dublin.

27. The Long Hall

51 South Great George's Street, Dublin 2, 01 4751590, no website

The Long Hall is more than a pub; it is a repository of social and cultural history in the way that a good museum should be. With its

red and white candy-striped canopies it is instantly recognisable, and could be easily mistaken for an antique Victorian barber shop or an old-world sweet shop. The pub derives its name from a long hallway which once ran along the left side of the pub. Until 1951 the main bar was a male-only space while women sat in the hall, which effectively functioned as an elongated snug. The Long Hall – now a protected structure – was built in 1877 by architects and builders Lockwood and Mawson and is replete with brilliant detail. The bar is divided into sections by elaborate wooden screens inlaid with gold leaf carvings, while the rear lounge and the front bar are separated by an art deco arch on top of which sits 'Old Mantel', an elaborate clock designed by Wekler and Schlegel which creates the illusion of a Victorian train station, a feature in many pubs built during the era. The initials 'POB', engraved in the wood panel below the clock, are those of former owner Patrick O'Brien, who arrived here in 1941. The walls are covered in an eclectic mix of paintings, engravings and posters, including representations of the dealings of the Russian Tsar Paul I with the Polish patriot Kościuszko and prints of Gainsborough ladies. Panels of art nouveau glass are to be seen over the entrance to the toilet. Nearby a poem titled 'In Praise of Guinness' reads: 'In Dublin there's a beauty that has no match/It's brewed in St James's, then thrown down the hatch.' The back bar is made of solid mahogany while the liberal use of concave and convex mirrors create the image of a larger premises, another architectural innovation commonly seen in Victorian pubs. Glittering chandeliers and extensive brass ornamentation complement the artwork, glass and wood.

When O'Brien died in 1970 he left the premises to his staff of six. Unfortunately, divisions arose and it was sold at auction to Gerald Houlihan – one of the six – in 1972 for £80,000. He later bought back much of the original contents at another auction held in the actual pub. Patrick O'Brien had travelled the world collecting antiques and had amassed an impressive collection by the time of his death; so extensive, in fact, that he had someone come in every Saturday to clean them. As well as the bar, an upper room in the building was chock-full of valuable objects, and old photographs show the collection even extended to the front window display. In the auction notes the contents of the pub were noted to contain 'original paintings by Jack B. Yeats, antique mirrors and glass, and wallpaper hand-painted in gold ... [and] old firearms, which decorate it in staggering numbers'. The sale lasted an entire day, with the antiques sold off from behind the bar, complete with a gavel-laden seller. Houlihan spent £10,000 buying back the contents he wanted, or, perhaps, could afford. That this was one-eighth the value of the premises gives an idea of the value and extensive nature of the collection. The eventual location of the Jack Yeats paintings is unknown, but the initiative of Houlihan is immediately visible in the pub. The afore-mentioned firearms hang on the walls on the left of the bar towards the back of the pub, while the grandfather clock, produced by a clockmaker in Temple Bar in 1881, is located on the wall to the left side of the long bar.

The pub has an interesting history. The turret-topped George's Street Arcade, directly across the street from the Long Hall, claims to have housed Europe's oldest shopping centre. The elaborate interior of the pub would certainly have met the high standards of the bourgeoisie shoppers because this was a wealthy part of Dublin in the 1880s.

The pub, like others in the city of a similar vintage, has a nationalist past. It was once owned by Joseph Cromien, one of the team behind the ill-fated Fenian Rising of 1867. Two other prominent plotters, John Devoy and Charles J. Kickham, also frequented the hostelry. Their plans came to nought when authorities got wind of the planned rebellion and closed down the premises.

The Long Hall is no stranger to fame. In the music video 'The Boys Are Back in Town' by Thin Lizzy, Phil Lynott is seen sitting at the bar – on the third stool along from the front door, to be exact – singing about spending his money in the old town. The writer Brendan Behan was his boisterous self here and, when in town, American rock star Bruce Springsteen is known to frequent the pub, while singer Rihanna was photographed leaving the pub some years ago. 2016 marked the 250th anniversary of this venerable establishment, and in 2017 it won the illustrious Dublin Pub of the Year award at the Irish Restaurant Awards. It is a true work of art, universally loved by all who set foot in it, and deserves its place in the canon of great Dublin and Irish pubs. For many it is the best pub of all.

28. The Lord Edward

23 Christchurch Place, Dublin 8, 01 4542158, www.lordedward.ie

This famous pub is named after Lord Edward Fitzgerald, the fifth son of the First Duke of Leinster and scion of a formerly powerful aristocratic and wealthy Irish Catholic family. Fitzgerald's ancestral home was Carton Hall in County Kildare, while his city base was Leinster House, now the seat of the Irish government. He also owned the now-demolished Frescati (sometimes spelled Frascati) House at Blackrock, a beautiful seaside Georgian pile.

Lord Edward reached a high rank in the English army and saw service in the American and West Indian colonies. He later served in the Irish Parliament as a result of his ancestry, but grew disillusioned when he realised it had no real power. When he became aware that the Irish government was nothing more than a puppet regime predicated on vote rigging, he was drawn to the United Irishmen, a political grouping agitating for armed insurrection against the British authorities. Along with Wolfe Tone, Napper Tandy and Robert Emmet, he helped plan the abortive rebellion of 1798 against the Crown. Rumbled by that ever-present bane of Irish rebels – the paid informer – he was arrested in his hiding place in nearby Thomas Street before the insurrection started. In resisting arrest he was severely wounded and later died of his wounds in Newgate Jail on the north side of the river Liffey. Fitzgerald was only 35 when he passed away, and is buried in Saint Werburgh's Church across the road from the pub. Ireland's foremost poet, William Butler Yeats, honoured the fallen insurrectionist in his famous poem 'September 1913':

Was it for this the wild geese spread
The grey wing upon every tide;
For this that all that blood was shed,
For this Edward Fitzgerald died,
And Robert Emmet and Wolfe Tone,
All that delirium of the brave?
Romantic Ireland's dead and gone,
It's with O'Leary in the grave.

The five-storey over-basement building that houses the Lord Edward pub was built in 1875, and was once part of a substantial terrace of residential houses, but now stands proudly alone. It was refurbished and reopened as a public house in 1901 by the Cunniam family, and remains a stark sentinel on the skyline in the heart of medieval Dublin under the imposing shadow of Christ Church Cathedral. The downstairs bar has a beautiful quarter-shaped marble counter, gas lighting, and an impressive 'confession box' snug, while the recently closed upstairs restaurant was the oldest dedicated seafood restaurant in the city. All is not lost for fish lovers, as Leo Burdock's, widely recognised as the best purveyors of fish and chips in the city, is just around the corner on Werburgh Street, where it has been a much-loved fixture since 1913.

The first floor cocktail lounge has a traditional beam ceiling and extensive stained glass, and was formerly the Cunniam's dining room, while the rooms above were bedrooms. The beautiful copper-topped bar counter has a stained glass depiction of 'The Meeting of the Waters', the confluence of the Avonmore and Avonbeg rivers in Wicklow, immortalised in the Thomas Moore poem of the same name. In 1989 the Cunniam family sold the pub to Dublin-born businessman David Lyster and his mother, Maureen, who still own it today. It is a pub that should not be missed if the visitor is on this side of the city, providing, as it does, a nice secular counterpoint to the theological attractions of the nearby Christ Church Cathedral.

29. Mary's Bar

8 Wicklow Street, Dublin 2, 01 6708629, www.marysbar.ie

Mary's Bar was going to happen in Dublin sometime. It is a recreation of a traditional spirit grocer, long the mainstay of the Irish pub scene, and a cause of much handwringing among temperance campaigners for many a long year. Here you can buy drink, food and hardware, all under one roof. If the visitor's needs stretch to a high-visibility jacket, nails or a dust mask, in addition to food and drink, then they have come to the right place. The customer can also chew on some retro confectionary while admiring the fixtures and fittings that help recreate the old-world atmosphere. Many urban pubs have played with the idea of licensed premises as home to haberdashery by including random items throughout the premises, but this is the first modern (or postmodern?) iteration that has taken the concept to its logical conclusion. The Irish Pub Company and similar concerns have designed and made pubs in Ireland for export to all corners of the globe for almost three decades now. As well as a Victorian model, the customer in Des Moines or Beijing can order a 'country shop' model with all the bells on, and have it up and running within months. While these facsimiles may be loaded with gewgaws, including groceries and tools, none of them ever function as a shop other than selling alcohol and food. Mary's is different: it has gone all the way. The establishment is located between a bank and a posh clothes shop, making this little piece of old Ireland all the more unexpected.

Mary's even claims a link to Michael Collins, as this building once housed the Wicklow Hotel, one of his many, many reputed haunts. To add further intrigue to the Collins link, there is a tale of murder. On 28 January 1921, Peter Doran, the head porter of the hotel, was shot dead in the hallway. Reputedly the murder was committed by some of Collins's henchmen because Doran was an informant to Colonel Hill Dillon, the deputy chief of British intelligence service in Ireland.

There is no doubting that this pub is a pastiche and, some would say, a gimmick. Yet, it is well realised, and could well be viewed as a mini living museum of social and cultural history, and, by this token, a valuable part of the tourist scene in Dublin. Perchance the visitor to Ireland cannot get into the hinterland to see the real thing the owners have thoughtfully brought a little piece of rural Ireland to the city, and, arguably, it is all the better for it. To add further value to this unique product, the owners have allowed the highly regarded Wow Burger franchise an outlet in the basement. It is a wonderful tribute to the evolution of the Irish pub.

Spirit Grocer

The Spirit Grocer Act of 1791 introduced a new type of pub license to Ireland; one that was to prove controversial. This license allowed the owner to sell spirits as well as ancillary commodities like meat, hardware, drapery or groceries. The legislation helpfully suggested tea, cocoa nuts, chocolate or pepper as possible commodities, in addition to the payment of a fee to acquire the license. The owner could sell any quantity not greater than two quarts as long as the alcohol was consumed off the premises. The licenses were much cheaper than a standard public house one and were easier to obtain. From the start they were viewed as opportunities for servants – women in particular – to imbibe under the false pretences of grocery shopping.

In February 1902 William Lawson presented a paper to the Irish Temperance Movement entitled *Licensing and Public House Reform in Ireland* in which he identified the problem of licenses to sell alcohol as a particular social evil. In Dublin 90 per cent of the trade was mixed, i.e. through spirit grocers, which he felt allowed women to put drink on grocery accounts and put the family into debt.

'It is quite common, in Dublin particularly, to have at one end of the counter a large pile of tea chests for females to go behind; to be hid from sight ... the dangerous secrecy arises from the want of suspicion of persons going into grocer's shops; other things may be wanted there, whereas going into a spirit shop nothing is supposed to be wanted except intoxicating drink.'

Spirit grocers were the backbone of the Irish rural pub until the advent of supermarkets and farmers' cooperatives, and the wider availability of transportation in the 1960s. They still exist, but in lesser numbers. Those few that remain in working order should be visited before they too go the way of the dodo in Ireland's ever-changing cultural landscape.

30. McDaid's

3 Harry Street, Dublin 2, 01 6794395, www.mcdaidspub.com

McDaid's of Harry Street (the street being named after Harry Dawson, a member of the family who developed much of this upmarket side of Dublin city) is a jewel in the crown of Dublin's literary pubs. The beautiful front bar is said to have been carved from the remnants of an old chapel once used by the Moravian Brethren – considered the oldest of all Protestant denominations – during the late eighteenth century and has tall, gothic-style windows and ornate stained glass. It is said the Moravians developed a tradition of standing corpses upright, hence the high ceiling. The building also once housed the city morgue.

Before it was purchased by John McDaid in 1936 the pub had been known as William Daly's bar. At that time it was very much a working-class bar, nothing as elaborate as the high Victorian splendour of the Long Hall or the Palace Bar. McDaid's is essentially one big room with a bar counter on the right-hand side (until the 1980s it was on the other side) and a small alcove at the back for those in need of a seat. The mosaic tiling behind the bar is distinctive, with representations of trams on O'Connell Street and assorted literary legends, but little of the ornate detail associated with many of the other famous old literary hostelries in the city. While there are antique mirrors, library books, old whiskey bottle boxes, used suitcases, bronze mixing tanks, and a huge old radio high above the main bar, it is the literary heritage of this wonderful pub that has put it on the map in Dublin city.

The original catalyst for McDaid's becoming a literary pub was the nearby location of *Envoy* magazine. The literary and arts journal, established in 1949 by John Ryan (subsequent owner of the Bailey pub), provided an outlet for a new generation of voices like Patrick Kavanagh and Brendan Behan. The magazine gave the 'peasant poet' Kavanagh a monthly column – and a regular income – from which he sniped at various targets in Irish life which did not meet his approval, including the Catholic Church, the Abbey Theatre and Radio Éireann – the state broadcasting company. McDaid's became the de facto office for *Envoy* and a favourite hangout for Kavanagh, Behan, Liam O'Flaherty and Anthony Cronin, amongst a host of other Irish literary characters.

In *Dead as Doornails*, a memoir of Dublin intellectual life in 1950s Dublin, the late Anthony Cronin described McDaid's as 'more than a literary pub'. Its strength, he wrote, 'was always in variety; of talent, class, caste and estate. The division between writer and non-writer, Bohemian and artist, informer and revolutionary were never rigorously enforced. The atmosphere could have been described as Bohemian-revolutionary.'

Owner John McDaid considered the pub an unlikely literary venue, as he told Professor Kevin C. Kearns: 'McDaid's was a dowdy little pub ... the plainest pub possible. That was one of the things in it I liked. And 90 per cent of the people in it were working class.' Paddy O'Brien, the famous barman who later moved to Grogan's after failing to buy the premises, agreed: 'McDaid's was nothing at all. It was a dreadful place ... just an ordinary pub with little snugs and partitions and sawdust and spittoons and you'd have elderly men in little groups spitting and all this sort of filth. And TB was rampant but you had to wash out those spittoons.'

In an era when the powerful Catholic hierarchy held Ireland in a vice-like grip it was different in McDaid's; there the bohemian spirits could move into a different world.

Patrick Kavanagh's biographer, Antoinette Quinn, wonderfully described Kavanagh's typical appearance in McDaid's: 'When he arrived unaccompanied, he would peer around the door for a couple of seconds, deciding which party to join, then stride in and make for his chosen group, attracting their attention with some general observation made in booming tones or launching into an anecdote.' Kavanagh was loud, argumentative and unconcerned with issues of personal hygiene, according to Quinn. On one occasion, when an apprentice barman spilt drink over the unpublished work of a young poet, Kavanagh told the employee that he was 'a useless barman but a fine judge of poetry'.

Kavanagh ultimately fell out with John McDaid over a financial misunderstanding. Paddy O'Brien knew Kavanagh's cheques would often bounce, and was smart enough not to attempt to cash them until he heard there was money to meet them. This arrangement continued for a number of years, but came to an abrupt end when John McDaid attempted to cash a bundle of cheques he found behind the till. When they bounced, he called Kavanagh to account. It brought their relationship to an end and McDaid's was forever more without the 'Monaghan ploughboy'.

Brendan Behan, another habitué of McDaid's, even took to bringing his typewriter to the pub in the latter days of his short life, and once turned up after spending a term in prison in 1939.

Kavanagh and Behan may have been the two writers most associated with McDaid's, but there were many others who passed through its portals. After the Second World War a substantial number of American students came to Ireland under the GI Bill. One such was the unusually named Gainor Crist, who was to become the inspiration for Sebastian Dangerfield, the main character in J.P. Donleavy's *The Ginger Man*. Anthony Cronin remembered Gainor Crist as 'a charming, bowler-hatted gent with a cane', a stark contrast to the ill-mannered waster Dangerfield comes across as in the novel. Donleavy came to Trinity College to study Natural Science, but ended up spending more time in the pubs. He was drawn to McDaid's and became friends with Brendan Behan and his infamous, and fantastically named, associate Lead Pipe Daniel the Dangerous. Behan was the first to read Donleavy's novel, after he broke into the writer's cottage in Wicklow, and, reputedly, famously said that 'this book is going to go around the world and beat the bejaysus out of the Bible'. Behan suggested some small changes, a couple of which Donleavy took on board. The character Barney Berry is reportedly based on Behan.

It was not just writers who made McDaid's a home from home. Erwin Schrödinger, a Nobel-Prize-winning Austrian physicist who had escaped Nazi Germany during the Second World War, worked at the Institute for Advanced Studies in Dublin until his retirement in 1955, and was wont to discourse on his favourite subject of wave theory in the evening time at McDaid's.

The hugely popular head barman, Paddy O'Brien, tried to buy the pub from McDaid when it went up for sale in 1972 but was unsuccessful when he was outbid by an English woman wishing to cash in on the literary, artistic and bohemian cachet attached to the pub by this time. The unfortunate O'Brien was unable to match the figure of £87,000 the premises eventually commanded. Disappointed with the result, O'Brien took his coterie of intellectual friends to Grogan's pub on the nearby South William Street. By then the major players of the literary pub era were gone to their eternal reward in the great pub in the sky. McDaid's may not be the literary haunt it once was, but it is still a great place to have a drink away from the nearby hustle of Grafton Street and imbibe the atmosphere of bygone days.

31. Mulligan's

8-9 Poolbeg Street, Dublin 2, 01 6775852, www.mulligans.ie

John Mulligan's is one of the great old pubs of Dublin, and has the much sought-after reputation of having one of the best pints – many say the very best – of Guinness in Dublin. It is a place of talk and laughter without the intrusion of modern technology, and represents all that is great about the traditional Dublin pub. Mulligan's is a simple space with a double bar at the front leading into a large seated area at the back on the right, but it has an ambience that is impossible to recreate. There is no singing allowed, and even over-animated discussions are frowned upon. Such is the traditional nature of Mulligan's that the *Evening Press* once saw fit to comment on the erection of the first ever Christmas decorations in the pub thus: 'Introducing Christmas decorations to Mulligan's is about the equivalent of burning incense in Christ Church.'

Mulligan's was first established on Thomas Street and moved to a succession of premises before opening on Poolbeg Street in 1854. Mick Smith bought the pub from John Mulligan in 1932, passing it on to his nephews Con and Tommy Cusack, who in turn passed it on to Tommy Cusack's sons, who still run it today. Mulligan's has a long and rich tradition of attracting customers from the creative arts and journalism. In the past it was a favourite of actors from the now defunct Theatre Royal; there is even a signed photograph of ill-fated American actress Judy Garland on the wall. The theatre was knocked down in 1962 and replaced with Hawkin's House, virtually universally reviled as the ugliest building in Dublin. Perhaps the man most associated with Mulligan's over recent decades was the now sadly deceased journalist Con Houlihan, whose sports writings are widely regarded to be without peer. A plaque on the wall includes a tribute from famous playwright John B. Keane: 'When he entered the sporting scene the cobwebs of bias and bigotry were blown away by the pure breath of his vision and honesty.'

It was with the *Irish Press* group that Houlihan first made his name in the national media, before later moving on to the *Independent* group of papers. Such was Houlihan's connection to the pub that he kept his wages in the safe here and kept money in a glass behind the bar to buy drink for himself and his friends. Famously, one of his tipples of choice was brandy laced with milk.

In 1964 the sweepstakes' organisers used the cachet of Mulligan's in an advertisement campaign: 'Joyce knew Mulligan's and his Select Bar and he trod the familiar streets on his way there. Mulligan's is part of Joyce's Dublin and the visiting much-travelled much-read tourists find their way there to pay homage, among them, in 1947, after leaving the Marines, John F. Kennedy.' Kennedy, who was working with the Hearst newspaper group at the time, came here in the company of Jack Grealish of the *Irish Press*, but he is not the only American to have left a lasting impression on Mulligan's. Billy Brooks Carr, from Houston, Texas, liked the Guinness and the company so much here that he had some of his ashes interred in the clock.

Mulligan's has made frequent appearances in film and television. It was used by American director Joseph Strick for scenes from his 1976 movie *A Portrait of the Artist as a Young Man*, based on the novel of the same name by James Joyce. Scenes from the hugely successful 1989 Neil-Jordan-directed *My Left Foot* were filmed here while it also appeared in *Hear My Song*, a biographical treatment of the life of Irish tenor Joseph Locke. The late Michael Dwyer, long-time chief film critic of the *Irish Times*, described the way the pub was used in the film as an iconic representation of Dublin: 'When the film moves from Liverpool to Dublin, one of the first shots of the city is outside Mulligan's pub as a priest in soutane walks by. This, we can assume, is an establishing shot in the same way as a red bus tells us we're in London or a shot of the Eiffel tower tells us we are in Paris.'

For literary aficionados the Joyce Room at the rear of the pub is so named in honour of its mention in Joyce's famous short story 'Counterparts'. Here Farrington ogles an English actress and is defeated by an acrobat called Weathers in an arm wrestle. It might just be the best Joycean pub connection of all.

Mulligan's is a wonderful slice of old Dublin and should definitely be on the itinerary of anyone seeking to sample the essence of a great city hostelry. For many surveyed it is the greatest of all Dublin hostelries.

Strange Things in Dublin Pubs

Every eighth day a bartender goes to the clock to 'wind up Billy' in Mulligan's pub. It is not the only unusual feature in a Dublin pub. The Clock pub on Thomas Street has an aviary in the beer garden, home to several rare species of bird. Toner's pub on Baggot Street takes a different approach to birds. A machine utilising predator bird noises goes off every eighteen minutes to keep away the local seagull population. In Fallon's pub in the Coombe there is a photo of a couple on their wedding day on the ceiling. The story goes that there was a regular who drank in the bar, sometimes to excess. When he had had enough he would sometimes fall off his chair. After falling backwards he would then look up at the ceiling, see his wedding photo and know that it was time to head home to his wife.

The Adelphi Bar on Middle Abbey Street has a beer for dogs. Snuffle is made entirely of natural ingredients and is alcohol free. Who said it's a dog's life?

(Until recently it was illegal to bring pets into a public establishment. Paragraph 22 of Regulation 25 of the Food Hygiene Regulations 1950 only allowed 'access for guide dogs, assistance dogs, companion dogs or dogs in training to become any of these'. In a statement released to the media after the introduction of Snuffle beer, Dogs Trust Ireland said that it was 'optimistic that this progressive step will be instrumental in helping Ireland to become more Dog Friendly'.)

32. Neary's

1 Chatham Street, Dublin 2, 01 6778596, www.nearys.ie

This late period Victorian pub, located just a few paces away from the hustle and bustle of Grafton Street, is difficult to miss on the short streetscape of Chatham Street. It is instantly recognisable by the fine red-brick exterior and the two beautiful cast-iron arms holding up lanterns with the name of the pub etched on them just outside the main entrance. It is an entrancing sight and a siren call to a bar that

should not be missed in Dublin city centre. The pub is named after Leo Neary, who combined the running of the pub with the duties of Honorary Consul of the Republic of Guatemala.

Chatham Street dates from 1785, and was named after the first Earl of Chatham, more famously known as William Pitt the Elder, Prime Minister of Great Britain and Ireland, or by others as 'The Great Commoner' because of his refusal to take a title until 1766 – an unusual choice in the class system of the time. He is referred to as 'Pitt the Elder' to distinguish him from his son William Pitt 'the Younger'. It may be considered somewhat strange that there is still a street in the capital city of a country named after the leader of an occupying force who quashed one of the most celebrated uprisings in its history, as Pitt the Elder was responsible for ending the 1798 Rebellion.

Griffith's Valuation identified the premises as a house and shop in 1853 owned by the Casserly family, and it is likely that it traded as the Casserly Tavern until 1887, when it was taken over by Thomas Neary. Apart from the beautiful outside lamps the pub is noted for its four inside gas lamps and the still functioning dumbwaiter, originally installed in 1957. Unlike some other Victorian pubs it is quite commodious and never seems to get overcrowded. The pink granite counter and the brass fittings give the pub a vaguely Parisian ambience, while the upstairs Chatham Lounge has a beautiful oval bar.

The pub's longstanding link with the theatrical community began when the Gaiety Theatre was built in 1871. With the rear door of the pub directly opposite the stage door of the theatre, it is little wonder that thespians have long frequented these beautiful premises, complimented by the uniform of white shirt and black bowtie worn by the staff. Comedian Jimmy O'Dea, a favourite with Dublin audiences for over forty years, considered Neary's his office. He always occupied the same seat when in residence and insisted on being addressed as Mr O'Dea. Actor Alan Devlin once infamously walked off stage in the middle of a show to go order a pint, made all the worse by the fact that his radio microphone was still live, allowing the audience to hear his conversation with the barman in the pub.

Albert Pierrepoint was possibly not as welcome to Neary's pub as those from the theatrical world. Pierrepoint was the last hangman employed in Great Britain and was sent to Dublin on occasion to take care of pressing business at Mountjoy Prison. On his visits it is said he liked to partake of a drink in Neary's, preferring a quiet snug to the hustle and bustle of the main bar.

In an area dominated by upmarket shops and restaurants, Neary's is a great place to take a step back from the madness and savour one of the best pints of Guinness in the city.

33. The Norseman

28 East Essex Street, Dublin 2, 01 6715135, www.norseman.ie

Of all the pubs in the Temple Bar this pub may have the most credible claim to something approaching a venerable history. Once called

Farrington's, after a character in James Joyce's short story 'Counterparts', it changed to The Norseman in recognition of its position at a junction where a wooden Viking figure was once located, and claims to have been the site of a drinking establishment called the Wooden Man Tavern. The full title of the current establishment is 'The Norseman Temple Bar 1696', celebrating the year the premises was first officially licensed. Joyce actually referred to the pub as J.J. O'Neill's in *Dubliners*. In 'Counterparts' Farrington enters the pub, goes downstairs to the toilet and then leaves to continue his pub crawl, eventually ending up in Mulligan's of Poolbeg Street.

This pub was formerly owned by John Morris, a well-known supporter of the arts, who often helped out those of limited means. It is unlikely there are many poverty-stricken artists in regular attendance now, given its location at the western fringe of Temple Bar. It is hard to believe the street was once famous for the number of coffee houses, as it is now almost completely given over to pleasure palaces of a different type. The Norseman is now three times the size it was a few years ago after a major expansion. Perhaps it might be somewhat easier to believe that this area of the city was once a red light district popular with students of the not far distant Trinity College. In general, the pubs of Temple Bar tend towards the expensive; the visitor pays a premium here, in the same way inflation is rampant at tourist haunts the world over. If Temple Bar has to be on the agenda this, along with the Palace Bar on the other side of the cultural quarter, might be the place to go.

Temple Bar

Located on the south bank of the river Liffey, Temple Bar is promoted as Dublin's cultural quarter. While it is home to some cultural institutions, including the Irish Film Institute (IFI) and the National Photographic Archives, the area is heavily dominated by pubs and restaurants. If the visitor wishes to see great Dublin pubs aficionados overwhelmingly suggest it might be better to keep away from the area, with the noble exceptions of the Palace Bar and the Norseman.

In 1609 Sir William Temple was appointed Provost of Trinity College and Master Chancery in Ireland and built a house on what is now the corner of Temple Lane and Temple Bar, the name of the main thoroughfare here. In 1656, John Temple, a son of William, added to the property and built a retaining wall to allow land reclamation ('Barr' - subsequently shortened to 'Bar' - was used to describe a raised estuary sandbank). The Liffey's embankment, which ran along the front of Temple's property, resulted in the name 'Temple's Barr'.

This area of Dublin city centre had fallen into dereliction by the 1980s, and the national bus company was planning to build a bus terminus here. After protests by heritage bodies, the Irish government came to the rescue and established the Temple Bar Trust in 1991. In place of the planned terminus plans were drawn up to create a cultural hub which would provide a home to museums, galleries and other cultural organisations. It was not envisaged that the area would become a party zone attracting hen and stag parties in great numbers but with the number of pubs in close proximity that is what happened. There are varying opinions on Temple Bar. For some, it is party central and a place to meet people from all corners of the world while listening to ear-splitting renditions of various types of Irish music. For others, it is an overpriced tourist trap. Temple Bar is also home to roughly 3,000 residents. There must be times when those who live here question their sanity in choosing the location.

34. O'Connell's Bar

29 South Richmond Street, Dublin 8, 01 4753704, no website

O'Connell is a surname that is associated with some great pubs throughout Ireland; there are outstanding bars bearing the name in Galway city; Ennis, County Clare; and Howth in the north of County Dublin. There has been a pub on this site since 1832, while the name of J. (Jeremiah) O'Connell has been above the door here since 1933. This is a bar with a great atmosphere and great prices, along with

a genuinely top pint of Guinness. The student of pub culture may recognise the outside, as it has appeared on many posters and calendars over the years. If a visitor wants to sample a bar that feels like it has been moved from a small town in rural Ireland to the capital city this would be a good choice. O'Connell's is an establishment where you will meet actual real-life locals among the eclectic clientele. The cheerful red and green colour scheme enhances the fuzzy glow of a dark evening with a few pints in this lovely pub. It is one not to be missed if a traditional pub is on your wish list.

35. O'Donoghue's

15 Merrion Row, Dublin 2, 01 6607194, www.odonoghues.ie

'They can have their fancy drink but when it comes to booze, you'll never beat the friends you'll meet in brave O'Donoghue's'.
                            From a poem on the wall in the pub

Of all the pubs in Dublin, O'Donoghue's was ground zero for the folk music revolution that swept the country in the 1960s. The Dubliners, led by the ginger-haired Luke Kelly and the impressively bearded Ronnie Drew, regularly held court here. It is still a Mecca for music lovers, with sessions seven nights a week. The walls of O'Donoghue's are covered in memorabilia of the halcyon days of the Dubliners and other ballad and folk groups of their generation. There is a poster advertising the Dubliners' 1976 German tour – 'Irland's Berühmte Folk Gruppe' – and a mirror on the side wall on which the group's faces are engraved.

The rules of geometry were completely ignored when this establishment was built and, with too much alcohol on board, the slanting walls and floors can induce a feeling of something like seasickness. The pub was bought by Paddy and Maureen O'Donoghue in 1934, who oversaw its development into a prime venue for music. While O'Donoghue's is most associated with the Dubliners, a plethora of famous Irish musicians and bands have graced the pub with their presence, including the Fureys, Paul Brady, Christy Moore and his band Planxty, Seamus Ennis, and traditional singer Joe Heaney.

Dessie Hynes purchased the bar in 1977 and ran it until 1988 (it was gutted by fire in 1985), continuing to nurture the great tradition of music, before selling it on to Oliver Barden and his family who, along with John Mahon, have kept it running smoothly ever since.

In keeping with the long musical tradition it is celebrated in song by writer and singer Andy Irvine on his 2007 album *Changing Trains*.

The alcove by the front window is the high altar for the musicians, around which the worshippers would gather every evening. Invariably some unsuspecting inhabitants of this alcove will have to abandon their seats when the musicians turn up; regulars know better than to sit in this space in the first place, and will try to secure stools elsewhere before musical proceedings begin. The pub also provides table service, a godsend in a bar this busy.

Like the nearby bars on Baggot Street, O'Donoghue's is a haunt of rugby and soccer followers when there is a game on in the nearby Aviva Stadium. It is also a favourite haunt of American rock superstar Bruce Springsteen when he comes to town. All is going swimmingly at O'Donoghue's; financial records show that the business doubled its profits in 2017 while high-profile guests during the year included *Aquaman* star Jason Momoa and Apple CEO Tim Cook.

36. The Old Stand

37 Exchequer Street, Dublin 2, 01 6777220, www.theoldstandpub.com

The Old Stand has stood in the same place, at the junction of Saint Andrew's Street and Exchequer Street, for over 300 years. Andrew's Street was once known as Hog Hill and was one of the most important streets in Dublin. Exchequer Street was given its name in 1776

from the old Exchequer which was sited here, having formerly been known from 1728 as Chequer Lane. In those days, Exchequer Street ran from George's Street onto Grafton Street; the eastern end of this street did not become Wicklow Street until 1838.

John Travere, a famous early patron of the pub, was a poor and lame cobbler known for his wit and cynicism who, during the 1760s, ran a shoe stall on Hog Hill, which attracted crowds to hear his unique humour. In the evening he continued his show in the Old Stand pub to the delight of patrons. The long and noble tradition of the bar-room wit is still one of the defining features of Dublin today, and it never takes long before the visitor is engaged in conversation by a talkative local.

Records show that in 1817 the site of the Old Stand was occupied by a spirit grocer established by James McClean. When John Cox took over in 1885 he concentrated on drink, and for over 40 years the premises traded as the Monaco. The Old Stand claims to have been used as a meeting place by the Irish Republican Brotherhood and Michael Collins during the War of Independence and, given that he had an office at nearby 4 Andrew Street (now the home of the Trocadero restaurant), it is likely that he did. A plaque and picture hang in the pub to commemorate his life.

Distinct features in the pub include a Welsh dresser made of Austrian wood and the impressive canopy island with its numerous horse brass fittings and collection of willow Wedgwood. Upstairs there are old paintings of Fishamble Street and Blackhall Place by Fergus O'Brien, as well as stunning photographs of the funeral of Kevin O'Higgins, the first Minister for Justice in the Irish Free State. O'Higgins was in charge of protecting the new state from subversive elements, sentencing to death 77 fellow Irishmen who had fought on the anti-Treaty side in the Irish Civil War of 1922–1923, including Rory O'Connor, who had been best man at his wedding. On 10 July 1927 O'Higgins was assassinated while on his way to Mass in Black-rock, County Dublin by three anti-Treaty members of the IRA for his role in those 77 executions during the Civil War. He was buried three days later in Glasnevin Cemetery following a state funeral. The funeral cortège stretched for over three miles along thronged and silent Dublin streets, with ten lorryloads of flowers behind the family wreaths.

For those who appreciated the witticisms of the late Jeffrey Bernard – once London's most famous journalistic drinker – this was his favoured tippling house of choice when in Dublin. The pub is named after a demolished stand at the international rugby ground formerly called Lansdowne Road, now the Aviva Stadium. It is a popular gathering point for rugby and horse-racing fans, and has established a reputation as a gastropub and trendy night spot for the well-heeled. If there is an international rugby match on in Dublin this pub will be packed.

For an older Irish pub it has unusually large windows, which make it a lot brighter than similar establishments of the same vintage. The stairs down to the men's toilet are steep and should be approached with caution. It is now owned by Colclough, Redmond and Michel Doran, members of a family who run a number of premises in the city, and who have been in the licensed trade for over 100 years.

Saint Patrick's Day and Pubs

Believe it or not, 17 March, in the middle of the Catholic festival of Lent, was an occasion of abstinence in the virtually theocratic early days of the Irish state. Saint Patrick's Day was once an alcohol-free zone. One of the very few places alcohol was available until the law changed in 1973 was in the Protestant-run member's lounge at the Royal Dublin Society (RDS) dog show. High attendance figures were guaranteed. Poet Patrick Kavanagh reputedly once rented a dog to get in, while it is said that his arch-nemesis, writer Brendan Behan, stole a poodle to gain admittance on another occasion. The celebrations now associated with the Irish national holiday were actually born in the United States. The first parade took place in 1762, when Irish soldiers serving in the British Army marched through Manhattan to a tavern, and it was 1931 before a parade took place in Ireland. In 1995 the Irish government, keen to maximise the commercial spin-off for the economy from the ever-growing tourist industry, introduced the five-day Saint Patrick's Festival.

According to Diageo, the average day sees 5.5 million pints of Guinness sold across the world; this rises to a remarkable 13 million on Saint Patrick's Day. It is almost impossible to believe that it was once a dry day in Ireland and the only option for tourists would have been to go to Mass, or to the dog show if they needed a drink.

37. O'Neill's

2 Suffolk Street, Dublin 2, 01 6793656, www.oneillspubdublin.com

Before the Normans got their hold on parts of Ireland the Vikings pillaged Dublin, and O'Neill's pub is built on the exact location of the Thingmote – the Dane's administrative headquarters. It was here they sat on top of a 40-foot-high mound and promulgated laws for their newly acquired territory, held sporting contests, and may even have hosted ritual sacrifices. The Thingmote was eventually levelled in 1681 by order of the chief justice and the soil used to raise the level of nearby Nassau Street to prevent flooding.

There is a lot of history attached to this venerable pub. The building was the residence of Robert, the Nineteenth Earl of Kildare in the early eighteenth century, while the section of the pub that now runs into Church Lane was once the location of a printing press where William Butler printed the *Volunteers Journal of the Irish Herald*, a paper censured in the British House of Commons in March 1876 for its nationalist views. Some years subsequently, *The Press*, a republican newspaper established by Arthur O'Connor – one of the leading supporters of Wolfe Tone and the United Irishmen – was printed in the same office.

From 1755 the Coleman family used a part of the building to run a grocer, tea, wine and spirits merchant. It was subsequently leased by the Hogan brothers, and bought by the O'Neill family in 1927. The pub has always benefitted from its high-profile location. The old Irish Parliament was located down Church Lane on what was then called Hoggen Green – now known as College Green – while the parish church of Henry Grattan's independent assembly was just across the road at Saint Andrew's.

The inside of O'Neill's is a labyrinthine warren of nooks and crannies, and it has long been a popular place for students of nearby Trinity College. Seats from the original Lansdowne Road sports stadium can still be found outside in the rooftop beer garden; there is even a plaque beside them certifying their authenticity. The snug is perhaps the biggest of all the beautiful examples in Dublin. It was here James Joyce set the first section of 'Counterparts' – a famous short story from his collection *Dubliners*.

Nowadays the pub is famous for its huge servings from the extensive carvery.

The Pubs in James Joyce's Dubliners

In *Dubliners*, James Joyce's celebrated collection of interlinked short stories, the author mentioned twelve pubs: Egan's of Abbey Street, Mulligan's of Poolbeg Street, O'Neill's of Suffolk Street, the bar of the Burlington Hotel, the Scotch House on Burgh Quay, Davy Byrne's on Duke Street, Dan Burke's of Baggot Street, the Bridge Inn in Chapelizod, Kavanagh's of

Parnell Street, McCauley's on Dorset Street, Corless's of Andrew Street and a fictional bar called the Black Eagle.

38. The Palace Bar

21 Fleet Street, Dublin 2, 01 6717388, www.thepalacebardublin.com

'The most wonderful temple of art'

Patrick Kavanagh

The Palace Bar on Fleet Street, dating from 1883, is one of the best preserved Victorian pubs in Dublin, and has a remarkably impressive literary pedigree. The four bronze plaques outside the pub, in memory of Patrick Kavanagh, Brendan Behan, Flann O'Brien and Con Houlihan, alert passers-by to the literary significance of the famous hostelry, while a few minutes inside should confirm its enduring attractions. At the start of the twentieth century, when many premises across the city were stripping out their antique interiors in an attempt at modernisation, the owners of the Palace Bar and Ryan's of Parkgate Street met to discuss the future: they agreed to leave their pubs unchanged in all their Victorian splendour. The result of their pact meant two of the most beautiful pubs in the city remained unsullied. The back bar of the Palace is arguably the most stunning space in a Dublin pub; the

comfortable rectangular space is a striking counterpoint to the narrow front bar.

With a beautiful high vaulted ceiling supported by Romanesque arches, it is best seen in the daytime when the intricacy of the craftsmanship can be appreciated in all its glory. This high Victorian style is also evidenced in the typically high bar counter. Sitting in one of the burgundy leather bucket seats with one of the best pints of Guinness in the country is a true pleasure on a bright Dublin day.

Honor Tracy, author of *Mind You, I've said Nothing! Forays in the Irish Republic*, came to Dublin with her partner in the 1950s to seek out 'Dublin intellectuals'. They went to the Palace and were joined by 'one of Dublin's major poets, with a thirsty look on his face'. It was most likely to have been Patrick Kavanagh. He was glad to depend on their kindness that evening, she wrote, because 'the confidence he felt in certain racehorses turned out to have been misplaced.'

Until 2006 the *Irish Times* newspaper was printed on Fleet Street, and the Palace Bar was a traditional gathering place for staffers. R.M. (Bertie) Smyllie, long-time editor of the paper, directed proceedings in a corner of the back bar termed 'the intensive care unit'. Most of the writers and artists were impoverished souls, and Smyllie was a meal ticket for many of them. On the wall of the back bar there is a large reproduction of a drawing by Alan Reeve titled *Dublin Culture* – the original hangs in the National Gallery. It depicts a group of literary figures at a Christmas party in the Palace; among the participants are Patrick Kavanagh, poet Austin Clarke, and the inimitable Flann O'Brien. O'Brien was a serial prankster and the Palace was the scene of one of his best known stunts. He once famously parked an engineless car outside the pub and sat in it. When challenged by a police officer he claimed he could not be prosecuted for propelling a mechanical vehicle because it had no engine.

Artists including Seán O'Sullivan, Patrick O'Connor and Harry Kernoff also frequented the Palace Bar; the latter sold his pictures from the wall. While Kernoff also exhibited in the Royal Hibernian Academy he sold dozens of his works in the pub, according to the current owner, Liam Ahearne. Kernoff was an underappreciated artist during his lifetime, and many of his works sold for tiny amounts. In the backroom of the Palace his work can be assessed at leisure. Two woodcut prints, high on the right-hand wall, portray pub scenes and are signed by Kernoff. One details a man playing an accordion-like instrument; the other is of three patrons in the bar. On the opposite wall there are two colourful portraits of women in headscarves and a pastel drawing of Irish actress Maureen O'Sullivan from 1944; all three are also by Kernoff. A good account of the artist's social life, including his regular evenings in the Palace, can be found in his diaries, which are housed in the National Library. Kernoff befriended many of the resident writers and even had the, perhaps dubious, pleasure of going on holiday with his fellow Palace aficionado Patrick Kavanagh. Where they found the money is unrecorded. Both were frequently broke and, according to Ahearne, there is a bounced cheque of Kavanagh's - for the sum of £1 and 10 shillings - in the basement of the pub.

There is a beautiful small snug at the front which, unusually, can be booked in advance. The Palace Bar was originally built in 1823 by a family named Hall. In the early 1900s it was taken over by the Ryan family from Tipperary, staying in their possession until sold by 'the widow Ryan' in 1946 for £27,000, an eye-opening sum at the time. It was bought by Bill Aherne - the famous 'mountainy man' from Rearcross, County Tipperary - and is now run by his son Liam and grandson William. The Ahernes are whiskey connoisseurs, and there are over 120 to choose from in the beautiful upstairs bar renamed the Whiskey Palace, including their own Palace Bar Irish Whiskey. The bottle's label depicts the exterior of the Palace and pays homage to its great literary past. Their 'Fourth Estate' single malt has a picture of R.M. Smyllie on the label. It is a fitting image in keeping with the pub motto: 'internationally famous for our intellectual refreshment'. Despite being on the edge of Temple Bar, this is a great and civilised place with an exceptional pint of Guinness and a soothing conversational hub. Among the whiskey bottles in the downstairs bar there is a sign which appropriately reads 'a bird is known by its song, a man by his conversation'. With no television the ebb and flow of conversation wafts continually through this national treasure. This pub should not be missed.

39. Peruke and Periwig

31 Dawson Street, Dublin 2, 01 6727190, www.peruke.ie

Set in a compact, three-storey Georgian house on Dawson Street, Peruke and Periwig has a beautiful Georgian, wood-panelled, ground-floor bar, in what was once an eighteenth-century peruke- and periwig-makers shop. The words 'peruke' and periwig' were used interchangeably to describe wigs made for men. They were typically made of long hair, often with curls on the sides, and drawn back on the nape of the neck. Toward the end of the sixteenth and the beginning of the seventeenth centuries the peruke was a distinctive fashion item among the aristocracy. (Louis XIII of France began wearing one in 1624). The many wigs displayed in this pub may bring this past vividly to life for some, but may not be everyone's idea of soothing decor.

A narrow staircase leads to the upstairs dining area which, decoratively speaking, is a feast for the eyes: rich, red velvet wall coverings and seating, gold braiding, fringed lamp shades, wood panels, heavy oil paintings, Staffordshire china dogs, and glittering chandeliers abound in the medium-sized, dimly lit area. The tables are on the small side, and some of the chairs are a bit low, but the food has received many plaudits since this elegant venue opened. It is, however, overwhelmingly, about the cocktails – and aficionados will not be disappointed. The extensive menu, presented in an impressive passport-like document, is largely based on musical themes: classical cocktails have been given new names to fit under a musical genre. Thus, a Charlie Chaplin, consisting of 'Plymouth sloe, Parfait Amour, apricot brandy, Peruke's plum shrub, lemon and cucumber', is rebranded as a 'Friends in Sloe Places' and placed under the 'Pop' heading. Musical diehards might find this disputatious, as the name is an obvious reference to the song 'Friends in Low Places', made popular by American country singer Garth Brooks.

Drinkers could hold a lengthy conversation on the classifications of the various drinks, as a further number are debatable inclusions in their respective categories. 'Pass the Dutchie' is the establishment's chosen title for a Margarita containing 'sage-infused tequila,

Earl-Grey-infused Cointreau, lime, honey, Kummel Wolfschmidt, whites, grapefruit bitters, Hellfire bitters and rimmed with basil salt' and filed under 'Blues'. Musical Youth, the band who released the reggae-inspired song with a contested reference to cannabis in the title, would surely scratch their collective heads to see it listed as a blues number. Such pointless debates aside, the cocktails here come highly recommended. It is owned by the same crew who run the equally well regarded Vintage Cocktail Club in Temple Bar, and has proven popular with those with deep enough pockets to sustain an assault on the bar. Cocktails are priced from €12 upwards.

40. P. Mac's

30 Stephen Street Lower, Dublin 2, 01 4053653,
www.facebook.com/pmacspub

Opened in 2013, P. Mac's, located on the corner of Digges Lane and Stephen Street Lower, is a craft beer pub par excellence, and a prime example of the evolution of the pub in Dublin in recent years. With over 30 drinks taps, board games aplenty, *Space Invader* and *Street Fighter* arcade machines, big dining tables, private booths, red candles, and great food, this well-located pub is in the vanguard of the new dispensation. The same team is behind Cassidy's on Westmoreland Street and the Blackbird in Rathmines. The large dining tables are a feature not traditionally associated with the Irish pub, and make this most sociable of institutions even more so. This is the world of the hipster, and the ambience, once sampled, is very seductive. It is instructive to see the level of provision and service new ventures must strive to provide in a hypercompetitive market. The selection of craft beer on offer in this establishment is exceptional, and it has set an exemplary high standard for all subsequent similar operations. The food is highly regarded, with the portions served among the biggest in the city, according to those in the know. There is nothing to want for in P. Mac's. It is a win-win situation for the customer. Such has been the popularity of this venture the owners opened a premises of the same name in Dundrum in November 2017.

41. The Porterhouse Central

45-47 Nassau Street, Dublin 2, 01 6774180, www.theporterhouse.ie

The Porterhouse in Temple Bar was the very first craft beer pub in Dublin. The late Oliver Hughes and his friend Liam LaHart opened their first Porterhouse in Bray, County Wicklow, in 1989, specialising in importing beers from around the globe, with an emphasis on Belgian produce. In 1996 they opened Porterhouse in Temple Bar, a move which was as far ahead the curve as it was possible to be. When they started brewing their own beer the two men created a media stir by naming one 'Weiserbuddy', based on the cheeky tagline that 'you would be wiser to drink one buddy'. Very few people foresaw the success that was to come their way.

In 1999 they opened a branch in Covent Garden, London, followed in 2004 by Porterhouse North in Glasnevin. Not content to rest on their laurels, the team subsequently established Porterhouse

Central on Nassau Street in a building that was also once the home of Jammet's Restaurant, the Berni Inn and Judge Roy Beans.

In 2011 they opened a franchise in the historic Fraunces Tavern in the financial district in Manhattan. The Porterhouse first became famous for its filtered, kegged and pressurised draught beers, and, from 2009, it developed a range of bottled beers. Over the years the group has run a number of successful festivals. In 2016 they rebranded the Glasnevin outlet as the Whitworth.

The Craft Beer Revolution

In 1980s' Ireland, the vast majority of pubs served Guinness, Smithwick's ale, Harp lager, and, maybe, Tennent's, or another branded lager. Later came other mainstream beers like Heineken, Carlsberg and Budweiser, and that, for many years, was the sum total of draught alcohol available in the vast majority of Irish pubs. No one could have foreseen the craft beer revolution of recent years. (However, the punter should not expect the plethora of beers on offer in many of Dublin's pubs in travels around rural Ireland, as there are still many establishments that have not – and may never – embraced the new revolution.) The late Oliver Hughes and Liam LaHart opened their first brew pub in Bray in 1989, but it did not survive. They persevered with their idea and opened the Porterhouse in Temple Bar in 1996, serving its own and a selection of imported beers. It was widely viewed as an eccentric move, but the chain now has four pubs in Dublin, and one each in London and New York. The men were the first to make pale ale in the country, and were the first to import beers like Erdinger and Herrnbräu to Ireland. Hughes and LaHart were at the vanguard of a movement that was slow in developing but has gained significant traction in recent years. Now there are brewing companies scattered across Ireland. Carlow Brewing Company (makers of O'Hara's beers), Galway Hooker Brewery, Dungarvan Brewing Company and Metalman Brewing are among the more prominent in an ever-enlarging field. In 2014 craft beers represented 1.5 per cent of beer sales by volume in Ireland. According to Beoir, a consumer organisation seeking to promote Ireland's native craft breweries, there were only 27 pubs serving craft beer in Ireland in 2010; by early 2014 there were 559. The Galway Bay Brewery is to the forefront of the scene and runs a number of bars in Dublin, including the Black Sheep and Against the Grain on Capel Street, the Brew Dock on Amiens Street, and Alfie Byrne's on Earlsfort Terrace. Other popular craft beer haunts include J.W. Sweetman on Burgh Quay, L. Mulligan Grocery in Stoneybatter, the Beerhouse on Capel Street, The Bull and Castle on Lord Edward Street, and the Headline on Clanbrassil Street. The majority of bars have widened their offerings in recent years to keep touch with the evolving drink scene. Perhaps the greatest sign of the success of micro-breweries has been the establishment of alternative brews by the large breweries.

42. The Porterhouse, Temple Bar

16-18 Parliament Street, Temple Bar, Dublin 2, 01 6798847,
www.theporterhouse.ie

43. Ruin Bar

33 Tara Street, Dublin 2, 01 4990509, www.ruinbar.ie

The Irish pub has been exported to all corners of the globe for many years, so it is a fair exchange for Dublin to experience a simulacrum of a drinking establishment from foreign shores. Ruin Bar is modelled on the 'ruin bars' of Budapest, which, in their strictest incarnation, are repurposed abandoned buildings. The phenomenon is most frequently dated to the establishment of Szimpla in District VII of the city, once the Jewish ghetto, in 2001. It is a fascinating scene.

This premises on Tara Street formerly housed MacTurcaill's and is under the command of the same wise heads who run Camden Exchange. Whether it manages to recreate the frisson of the edgy bar scene along the banks of the Danube in the once capital of the Austro-Hungarian Empire is a matter of personal opinion. Others might suggest that importing a conceptualisation of a drinking space from another culture into Ireland is akin to bringing coals to Newcastle. Whatever of that argument, the food, artwork and drinks menu are all highly impressive in this brave new world. It is a particularly spacious venue, a world removed from the tight, cosy spaces of the vast majority of traditional Irish pubs. Those of the old school might consider this anathema, but the public house is a democracy, and there should be one to suit every taste. This might be the one for you.

44. Searson's

42-44 Upper Baggot Street, Dublin 4, 01 6600330, www.searsonsbar.ie

When acclaimed poet Patrick Kavanagh lived at nearby 62 Pembroke Road this was often his first stop of his alcohol-fuelled day, as he made his meandering way to the city centre, composing some of the most beautiful poetry ever written in Ireland. Searson's was also a stop on his way home, when the effects of the alcohol consumed during the day may have improved his mood, particularly if R.M. Smyllie, patron of the arts and editor of the *Irish Times*, had paid

his customary £1 for the pleasure of acquiring Kavanagh's latest creation. During his time residing in Pembroke Road Kavanagh fell in unrequited love with Hilda Moriarty, who later married the swashbuckling Minister for Education Donagh O'Malley, originally an architect from Limerick. Despite the frequent love poems Kavanagh wrote to woo Hilda her head was turned by the prominent politician. It was after he heard of her engagement that he penned what many consider one of the most beautiful love ballads of all time, 'Raglan Road' – originally called 'Dark Haired Miriam Ran Away'. When sang by the inimitable Luke Kelly of famed ballad group the Dubliners it became a transcendent work of art. Kavanagh was a genius, but he was also a difficult man to get along with, and eventually he fell out with the owner of Searson's, largely because of the altercations he had with Brendan Behan on the premises.

Baggot Street was originally named after Baggotrath, a manor granted to Robert Bagnod in the thirteenth century, located on the site of the current junction of Waterloo Road and Baggot Street. It was later destroyed in the nineteenth century. A pub was first opened at this site by Henry Tobin in October 1845 when he established a spirit grocer. It was subsequently purchased by William Davy, who gave it an elaborate Victorian makeover in 1890. After Davy's death in 1920 the pub was sold to William and Michael Searson. The Searson family, originally from Garrett's Mill near Killea in the north of County Tipperary, were serial publicans who also owned pubs in South Richmond Street, Portobello, and the seaside suburb of Blackrock. William Searson passed away on 20 August 1959, and the pub was sold to the Hardy family at public auction for £30,000 in 1961. 'Publin' was very impressed when he described the pub in his 1969 guide: 'The clientele is not what you expect to find in a quiet corner of an old city. It is a big, booming, slightly unbelievable pub but it's worth a visit just to see how the other half lives – or, if you're in that half yourself, to remind yourself of your status.'

This landmark premises is now owned by serial publican Charlie Chawke, who gave it an extensive makeover after he bought it when the Thomas Reid Group went into receivership. It is heaving whenever there is a sporting occasion in the nearby Aviva Stadium.

45. The Stag's Head

1 Dame Court, Dublin 2, 01 6793687, www.stagshead.ie

The Stag's Head, with its mahogany timberwork and Connemara marble- and granite-topped bar, is a true step back in time, and is, without doubt, one of the most beautiful pubs in Dublin. While there is a record of a pub on the site dating back to 1770, and John Bull's Albion Hotel was flourishing here during the 1830s, the extant building was designed by architect A.J. McLoughlin in 1895 and built by George Tyson – his initials decorate the iron clock and the wrought iron of the exterior – whose mission was to create an establishment which would bear 'favourable comparison with the best establishment of its kind either in London or any other part of England'.

The Stag's Head is a beautiful three-storey building of Dublin redbrick with a frontage of limestone and polished granite columns. The name of the pub adorns another piece of granite in distinctive gold lettering. Lest any punter be still unsure of their location, there is another stag's head, this one with gilded antlers, hanging over the front entrance.

The Stag's Head was the first pub in Dublin to be fitted with electric lighting, controlled by a switchboard behind the bar, although it is still so dark it sometimes seems there are no lights on, giving the pub a uniquely religious feeling. The stag mounted behind the bar – some say it is a moose – supposedly ran its head into the original hostelry during the 1770s while trying to escape its fate as a dinner dish for the grandees of Dublin Castle. Those who know their moose from their stags point to the length of the nose to support their opinion that the fourteen-point antlered head is, indeed, that of a moose. Around the inside of the pub there are stag representations aplenty, including mantle shields, and a mosaic at the back entrance. The beautiful snug at the end of the bar with its own entrance – this one is called the Smoke Room – is floodlit by six circular leaded windows reflected into the space by the inlaid mirrors

in the wood panelling, making it seem bigger than it actually is, a common optical illusion used by Victorian designers.

True to its elevated ranking in the hierarchy of great Dublin pubs, it has always had a strong attraction for the literary and artistic set. James Joyce was a fan, and it has been used as a film set for the Brendan Gleeson film *The Treaty* and the highly successful *Educating Rita,* starring Michael Caine and Julie Walters.

The Stag' Head, like so many the pubs of its era, claims an important historical link – once again with Michael Collins. Due to its proximity to Dublin Castle it was, it is claimed, another of the freedom fighter's favoured haunts during the War of Independence. Certainly the level of lighting that exists in this hostelry would have suited his surreptitious activities.

In 1978 the Stag's Head was purchased by the Shaffrey brothers from Cavan, who subsequently sold it on to the Louis Fitzgerald group. It is another of those Dublin pubs used to the comings and goings of the great and the good, and it would appear the staff are unfazed by celebrity. The American film director Quentin Tarantino turned up here one night but was not admitted because the pub was closing. (He returned the next day to have lunch.) It really is that type of pub, and is a must-visit of any tour of great Dublin hostelries.

46. The Swan

58 York Street/Aungier Street, Dublin 2, 01 4752722,
www.theswanbar.com

The Swan is a classic example of a great Victorian pub, and is another drinking establishment in Dublin that played its part in the bid made by Irish freedom fighters to escape the tyranny of British colonial rule. It was occupied during the 1916 Easter Rising as it sat close to Jacob's biscuit factory, which was captured by rebels under the command of the subsequently executed leader Thomas MacDonagh. The Swan was one of the last requisitioned garrisons to surrender. Irish Volunteer Michael Molloy described events when the rebels were ordered to evacuate the premises: 'Orders were also given that we were to burrow through from Jacob's to a public house at the corner facing Aungier Street. We had two masons in our party and the burrowing was made easy. Strict instructions were given that no Volunteer was to take any drink from the public house. And although I am not a drinking man myself I must say that this order was strictly obeyed.' The pockmarks of artillery fire were visible for many years on the walls of the premises.

The Swan claims to have been on this site since 1661, having replaced a previous medieval inn. Aungier Street took its name from Sir Francis Aungier, who developed what was then Ireland's widest street, long since bypassed by O'Connell Street, the main street in the city centre. While it began trading as The Swan in 1723, the pub now standing was built by Thomas F. O'Reilley in 1897, and has many exceptional Victorian features, including an old cash desk, solid Scottish granite bar counter, original copper alloy pouring taps, a hand-carved teak back bar, mounted barrels for pouring spirits, and a beautiful mosaic floor.

The pub is now in the hands of Ronan Lynch, whose family bought the premises in 1937. It made the news in 2013 when it voiced opposition to the Twelve Pubs of Christmas. Lynch was vehement in his opposition when he spoke to Áine McMahon of the *Irish Times*: 'We were getting feedback from our customers that they weren't happy about large crowds coming in. People were coming in and smashing glasses and being a bit of a nuisance. When you have 30 people coming into a small Victorian pub like ours, it can't really cope with the large numbers. The decision to stop "12 pubs" people coming in

is because of a combination of customer feedback and the behaviour that accompanies 12 pubs.' The Lynch family believe that a good pub should be treated like 'a party in the sitting room of your house'. Young people, Ronan Lynch claimed, often fail to understand 'pub etiquette' but he was at pains to point out that he was referring to only some of the younger generation: 'I'm not tarring everyone with the same brush but it is typically the older generation who can come in, sit down, have a chat and have three or four drinks. A problem with the younger generation now – and it's not all of them – is that they aren't used to this way of drinking in a pub. Getting drunk is the end game for many and that ties in with the 12 pubs .... We're a small pub without a bouncer. The bigger venues can take these crowds.'

The Swan has a strong sporting pedigree. John Francis 'Seán' Lynch co-owns the pub with his son Ronan, and is a former Irish international rugby player, having been capped fifteen times between 1971 and 1975. He was also a member of the British and Irish Lions team which toured New Zealand in 1971, and has the proud record of playing all four tests against the All Blacks – the name given to the always formidable New Zealand team. Lest the punter be in any doubt of Seán's sporting prowess, there is a fine collection of international jerseys and rugby paraphernalia on prominent display.

Despite being near Temple Bar, this is a pub where locals and tourists mingle and it is one of the best examples of high Victoriana left in Dublin. As John Lynch of the *Irish Times* wrote, when reviewing what he considered the best pubs in Ireland, 'it fulfils all their [tourists'] expectations of the Dublin drinking experience, minus the cringeful tat'.

The Twelve Pubs of Christmas

The title of this relatively recent Irish 'tradition' is self-explanatory. Participants take a drink of their choice in twelve different premises on one day or night, or both, during the Christmas season. As part of the tradition, participants tend to wear the most outlandish Christmas sweaters they can lay their hands on; the visitor will always recognise a participating group. Typically the merry team will have different rules for different pubs, enforced by a leader, sometimes with a whistle. For example, participants might have to drink with their left hand only in one pub, and be denied permission to go to the toilet in the following establishment. If the rules are broken, the guilty party will, inevitably, be required to drink more. There are many internet sites suggesting sets of rules: swap shoes with someone before the next drink, no speaking in one pub, not being allowed to hold your own drink so that someone else must feed it to you, not being allowed to put your drink down, being required to hug a stranger, having to drink only sitting on the floor, crawl to a pub or, somewhat ludicrously, call the barman or woman 'Guinness'. In this case the customer orders a drink by saying 'a pint of Heineken please Guinness' and, if you are given both, you must drink them.

Given that the whole enterprise inevitably results in the consumption of a large amount of alcohol, it is not a tradition universally appreciated by other customers or, in some cases, by publicans themselves. Some pubs have banned the custom outright, and signs refusing admission have become increasingly commonplace in recent years. There has long been widespread criticism of the prevalence of binge-drinking in Ireland by health professionals, which, inevitably, led to increasing criticism of the twelve pubs tradition in the media. For those who have campaigned against and complained about the danger of binge-drinking in Irish culture, the arrival of this newly formed 'tradition' must have seemed like a fully fledged nightmare. Nor is it a cheap night out – particularly in Dublin. If a visitor is insistent on experiencing the 'tradition', the 'Baggot Mile' route might be worth considering. Starting by the Grand Canal at Wellington's pub, the participants wend their way towards Saint Stephen's Green, visiting twelve pubs along the way.

47. Toner's

139 Lower Baggot Street, Dublin 2, 01 6763090, www.tonerspub.ie

The plain and unpretentious snug in Toner's is one of the best loved in the city. It was here that scenes from the Sergio Leone film *A Fistful of Dynamite*, also known as *Duck, You Sucker!*, was filmed. The pub is the setting for a flashback scene, where Seán Mallory, an Irish republican explosions expert hiding out in Mexico, remembers why he is on the run from the British authorities. The scene is filmed in slow motion with a score by Ennio Morricone. There is nothing in the snug to commemorate the film, but for fans of the movie there is a photograph of the director holding a gun on the main wall in the bar. In the snug there are a number of photographs of the winning Dublin Gaelic football teams of the modern era, and a sign announcing it as the 'snug of the year 2010' as voted by the 'Irish public in association with Powers whiskey'. If the visitor is lucky enough to find it free, it would be a travesty not to stop for a libation.

Toner's location in the heart of the affluent south side of the city centre attracts a strong corporate and professional crowd, and makes it a haunt for opinion shapers and media types.

Toner's is said to be the only pub ever visited by poet W.B. Yeats. When brought here by fellow literary heavyweight Oliver St John Gogarty, he, supposedly, sipped his drink, took one look around, and decided he had seen enough. He reputedly said: 'I have seen a pub. Will you kindly take me home?' The raucous atmosphere of the pub was obviously not in keeping with the ascetic interests of the esteemed poet. Despite this, Yeats later referred to his attendance of Dublin pubs in a BBC broadcast of his poetry. He claimed the rhythms of singing and chanting he had heard in Irish pubs would help alleviate the monotony of hearing poetry on radio. If both sounds could be married together, he opined, it would be the perfect match. As with other Yeatsian stories, the truth is elusive. Despite his reputed aversion to public houses Yeats was known to drink in Ye Old Cheshire Cheese pub, just off Fleet Street in London, where the Rhymer's Club – an association he co-founded with Ernest Rhys in 1890 – regularly met until 1904.

Toner's was originally constructed in 1818, and the drawers behind the bar are a reminder of its early days as a spirit grocer; the uneven flagstone floor is a further indicator of its venerable nature. The pub was opened as a grocer and wine merchant by Andrew Rogers, who ran it until his death in 1859 – the lane bordering the side of the pub is called Rogers' Lane – when it was taken over by inappropriately named publican William F. Drought, who was later succeeded by John O' Neill (1883–1904) and James M. Grant (1904–1923). It was to O'Neill that a grant of arms from Dublin Castle was given in 1886, proclaiming him grocer to the Lord Lieutenant, the highest office holder in the colonised country. It was not until 1923 that the pub became the property of James Toner, the fifth and by far the longest lasting owner. Toner ran it until 1970, when it was purchased by solicitor Joe Colgan, who in keeping with tradition – as well as being a sound commercial decision – retained the name. In 1987 it was purchased by current owners Frank and Michael Quinn. The yard bar (complete with a bird scarer which goes off every eighteen minutes) brought a whole new dimension to the premises when it opened in 2012, and is regarded by many as the best beer garden in the city.

In 2014 Toner's won the title of 'Best Traditional Pub' in the National Hospitality Awards and the following year it took the 'Dublin Bar of the Year' at the Sky Bar of the Year Awards – both highly sought after baubles in the industry. As well as the stock drawers and flagstone floors, the glazed cabinets filled with ancient curios, elaborate mirrors, and brass bar taps all contribute to the museum-like appearance of these beautiful premises. If that was not enough, the pub also has an excellent function room upstairs. This is the type of pub which investors have sought to replicate across the world, with varying degrees of success. It is the real thing.

48. The Vintage Cocktail Club

15 Crown Alley, Temple Bar, Dublin 2, 01 6753547,
www.vintagecocktailclub.com

The definition of a cocktail is simple: a mix of two or more drinks and flavourings, one of which must be alcohol. However, as with so many of these things, the origin of the term is disputed. The *Oxford English Dictionary* cites the word as originating in the United States, with the first recorded use of cocktail as a beverage, possibly non-alcoholic, appearing in the *Farmer's Cabinet* of 28 April 1803, while the first definition of cocktail known to be an alcoholic beverage, it suggests, appeared in the *Balance and Columbian Repository* newspaper in New York in 1806, when editor Harry Crosswell answered his own question, 'What is a cocktail?': '*Cock-tail* is a stimulating liquor, composed of spirits of any kind, sugar, water, and bitters – it is vulgarly called *bittered sling*, and is supposed to be an excellent electioneering potion, in as much as it renders the heart stout and bold, at the same time that it fuddles the head. It is said also, to be of great use to a democratic candidate: because a person having swallowed a glass of it, is ready to swallow anything else.'

However, there is a whole other school of thought on the etymology of 'cocktail'. In olden days it was the custom to dock the tails of horses not considered thoroughbreds. These less than

perfect equine specimens were known as cocked tails, later shortened to cocktails. The term became used to describe a person who
was seen as ill-bred and not of pure stock. Those who support this
version of the origin suggest the word came to be used to describe
a drink corrupted by mixing different liquids together. This was
not a thoroughbred drink, but rather an inferior product – a mere
'cocktail'. This is not the only other school of thought. In his 2007
book *Imbibe!*, David Wondrich speculated that 'cocktail' could be a
reference to a practice whereby a horse was given a ginger supposi-
tory to 'cock its tail up and be frisky'. The mind boggles.

The first published bartenders' guide to include cocktail recipes
was the 1862 *How to Mix Drinks*, subtitled *The Bon Vivant's Companion*,
by 'Professor' Jerry Thomas. As well as recipes for punches, sours,
slings, cobblers, shrubs, toddies, flips and a variety of other mixed
drinks, the author provided ten recipes for 'cocktails'. A key ingre-
dient differentiating cocktails from other drinks in his compendium

was the use of bitters. Mixed drinks popular today which follow this original meaning of 'cocktail' include the Old Fashioned and Manhattan.

Having ebbed and flowed in popularity over the decades, it is now without doubt the age of mixologists and their ever more elaborate concoctions. The Vintage Cocktail Club is widely regarded as the best of its kind in Dublin, and is enormously popular. The cocktail menu is vast, with a large section of it arranged chronologically, explaining when the particular drink first saw the light of day. Not alone is time spent here a pleasant drinking experience, it is also a history lesson. The studious drinker can learn, for example, that absinthe first became popular in the 1400s, although this information might be soon forgotten seeing as the Vintage serves a drink called 'Absinthe Minded' – a mixture of 'La Fée Blanche, Johnny Walker Black, Hayman's sloe gin, Cherry Heering, fresh citrus, with a grapefruit twist'. The first Martini came on the scene in 1833, the menu notes; the version served here calls for 'equal parts Jensen's Old Tom Gin and VCC Sweet Vermouth, Angostura Orange Bitters, with orange oils'. Four years later, its close cousin, the Dry Martini, came along. The Vintage serves one consisting of '5/2 parts Tanqueray No. Ten Gin to VCC Dry Vermouth, with lemon zest or olives'. The famous Manhattan cocktail came on the scene in 1874; a mixture, in this case, made up of 'equal parts Bulleit Bourbon and Carpano Antica Formula Sweet Vermouth, Angostura Bitters, with orange oils and cherry'. On and on it goes. The final section of the unbelievably lengthy menu outlines the venue's own cleverly named concoctions. They have a 'Falls Road Flip' containing 'Mozart White Chocolate Liqueur, Calvados V.S.O.P. Apple Brandy, grapefruit and passion fruit, Cranberry Bitters, fresh citrus, one whole egg, with a passion fruit coin', or, if that does not take the patron's fancy, there is a 'Tequila Mocking Bird', a mixture of 'Don Julio Reposado Tequila, Poire Williams Brandy, violet and walnut, fresh citrus, egg whites, with an apple fan'. Bookings for this brave new world come in two-and-a-half-hour blocks but, thankfully, extensions are available. It could be a long night. The attentive patron could spend nearly that amount of time reading the menu alone.

49. Whelan's

25 Wexford Street, Dublin 2, 01 4780766, www.whelanslive.com

While there are records of a pub on this site dating back to 1772, its purchase by Gary Whelan and Ian Keith in 1989 represented a milestone in the history of live music in Dublin, and Ireland. Whelan, an Irish actor who had lived in London for a number of years, and who starred in *Eastenders* and *Ballykissangel*, returned to his native Wexford Street with big plans at a time when the economy was in the doldrums. The duo renovated the premises but, unfortunately, debt forced the pair to sell to Liam Hanlon two years later. Fortunately, Hanlon went on to oversee the development of the venue into one of the city's premier live music venues.

The music venue was originally a warehouse and was purchased at the same time as the front bar. The flywheel used to raise and lower goods is still visible above the upstairs window. Adding an artistic touch to proceedings, the murals in the balcony bar are reproductions of Michelangelo's work on the Sistine Chapel in Rome. Continuing the artistic theme, the ground floor of the music venue features murals reproduced from the *Book of Kells*. The three main murals – hidden by the stage curtain at night – depict three of the four evangelists: Mark as the lion, Luke as the calf and John as the eagle. (The calf also appears in the front bar.) These panels are taken from the front pages of the gospels, while the Whelan's logo itself is one of the many feline monsters which occur throughout the Good Book. The Stone Man, a life-size statue of a lone drinker propped against the Stone Bar, adds a further artistic dimension to the establishment. This unusual edifice is made with fired wood chips, a type of complex papier mâché.

The list of performers and famous gigs in Whelan's over the years is mind-boggling: Jeff Buckley, Nick Cave, David Gray, Christy Moore, Damien Rice, Artic Monkeys and the Magic Numbers have all entertained audiences here. Successive music programmers David Allen, Derek Nally, Leagues O'Toole and David Allen again have kept things interesting for nearly thirty years. Whelan's has been under the ownership of Frank Gleeson since 1999, and there is

now a second performance space upstairs, called the Parlour, which holds 200 people.

Whelan's featured prominently in the film *P.S. I Love You*, starring Hilary Swank and Gerard Butler, based on the novel of the same name by Irish author Cecilia Ahern. It is best remembered for the performance of 'Galway Girl' and the line 'Denise, take Holly to Whelan's, my favourite pub. There's beautiful music to be heard, beautiful people to be around.' If live music is required Whelan's is a must on any itinerary of Dublin pubs.

Dublin City Centre North

1. The Church

Junction of Mary Street and Jervis Street, Dublin 1, 01 828 0102,
www.thechurch.ie

Saint Mary's Church of Ireland was the first church in the city to be designed with galleries, a feature which makes this a great place to people-watch now that it has been converted into a pub and night club. Designed in 1697 by Sir William Robinson, the foundation stone was eventually laid in 1700. Like many churches in Dublin it never received its intended spire, but has a foreshortened tower at the west end to compensate. The church is galleried around three sides, with an organ placed opposite the main window, while the ceiling is barrel-vaulted with an elaborate pattern of plaster-work. The galleries are supported on octagonal columns, which also underpin the roof. In 1742, George Frederic Handel famously performed his epic musical composition *Messiah* in public for the

first time on Fishamble Street, but before that he regularly practised on the Renatus Harris-built organ in this beautiful building.

In 1747, John Wesley, founder of the Methodist Church, gave his first sermon in Ireland here to what he termed 'as gay and senseless a congregation as ever I saw'. The Archbishop of Dublin was not impressed either, and Wesley was banned from speaking in every church in the archdiocese. The Dublin Methodist Council subsequently placed a plaque in the church to commemorate the event; it was later moved to Dublin Central Mission on Lower Abbey Street after Saint Mary's closed. Arthur Guinness, founder of the brewing empire, was married here in 1761, and satirical writer Jonathan Swift was among the countless parishioners who attended services over the years. The Irish playwright Seán O'Casey – author of *The Plough and the Stars*, *Juno and the Paycock* and *The Shadow of a Gunman*, amongst other plays – was baptised here in 1880, as was Theobald Wolfe Tone, the leader of the failed 1798 insurrection, 100 years previously. The theatrical link did not stop with O'Casey because Richard Brinsley Sheridan, author of plays *The Rivals*, *The School for Scandal* and *A Trip to Scarborough*, was also baptised here in 1751.

The graveyard is home to a number of notables, including Mary Mercer, founder of Mercer's Hospital, the seventeenth-century philosopher Francis Hutcheson, and Lord Norbury, the infamous hanging judge who sentenced patriot Robert Emmet to death. The original church yard was converted into what is now a public park called Wolfe Tone Square; the old gravestones can be seen at the southern end of this space.

Due to falling numbers of parishioners, the church closed its doors and was deconsecrated in 1986. It was then variously used as a home decoration store, a home for the Greek Orthodox Church and a dance school before falling into considerable disrepair; it was purchased and restored in 1997 by developer John Keating. The building needed an almost decade-long period of renovation to get it back into the condition it is in now. The old altar is now a performance area for bands, while a new entrance was knocked out along the northern side of the building, making the southern side (along the park) the most representative of Robinson's original design. Opened in December 2005, it is a protected structure, and, after being sold in 2007, now trades as the Church Bar and Restaurant. Aesthetically it is one of the most beautiful and expansive pubs in the city. The floor of the former Adelphi theatre on Abbey Street – it later became a cinema – is now located in a connecting hallway in the premises. Among the famous names that played the old Adelphi theatre were The Beatles, Fleetwood Mac, The Rolling Stones, Bob Dylan, The Beach Boys and Johnny Cash.

The conversion and refurbishment of this Dublin landmark was acknowledged at the Dublin City Neighbourhood Awards 2006, when it won first prize in the category of 'Best Old Building'. In an area of frenetic commercial activity, this hostelry provides a welcome and peaceful retreat for those who enter its impressive portals.

Guinness

Nobody thinks of Irish pubs without casting a thought to the black stuff; the 'pint of goodness' is as synonymous with Ireland and its pubs as America is with apple pie. Yet porter – the name given to the class of beer that Guinness belongs to – is not an Irish invention at all. While Arthur Guinness began the first mass production of this distinctive beverage – made from water, roast barley extract, hops and brewer's yeast – at his brewery in Dublin, it had first seen the light of day in London, where it was popular with porters working in the city's markets, hence the name. The draught form of the drink is characterised by a thick creamy head, sometimes called the 'Pope's collar', and is created by the addition of carbon dioxide and nitrogen when it is being poured, an innovation introduced in 1959. Despite declining sales since 2001, Guinness is still the best-selling alcoholic drink in Ireland. In 2016 Diageo made Guinness suitable for consumption by vegetarians and vegans when they introduced a new filtration process that avoids the need to use isinglass from fish bladders to filter out yeast particles. Despite having a reputation as a meal in a glass, a pint of Guinness actually only contains 198 calories. Pouring Guinness has acquired the reputation of being somewhat of an art form, characterised by the 'two-pour step ritual', or 'double pour'. Diageo advise that this should take exactly 119.5 seconds to achieve. To begin the pour, the server holds the glass at a 45-degree angle below the tap and fills the glass three-quarters full. After allowing the initial pour to settle, the server fills the remainder of the glass until the head forms a slight dome over the top of the glass.

Advertising has played a huge part in the success of Guinness, and it would be hard to leave the country without taking home some representations of the classic John Gilroy artwork, first created in the 1930s and 1940s. It was Gilroy who created the famous toucan that adorned the iconic 'Guinness Is Good for You' posters created by the S.H. Benson advertising company. The harp, synonymous with Guinness advertising, was modelled on the Trinity College Harp, designed by Benjamin Lee Guinness in 1862. Close observers will notice that the harp faces right to distinguish it from the harp on the Irish coat of arms, which faces left. Guinness once owned and managed a group of pubs in Dublin including the Sheaf O'Wheat in Coolock (now the Cock and Bull), the Clonsilla Inn, the Cherry Tree in Walkinstown and Doherty's of Harold's Cross. The company subsequently sold them off and, unlike Britain, there is no system of tied houses in Ireland.

Roughly 40 per cent of Guinness brewed annually is sold in Africa, while the drink entered the Indian market in 2007 and China in 2017. The United Kingdom is the only state to consume more Guinness than Ireland (total volume), with Nigeria and the United States occupying third and fourth places in the worldwide consumption league. A visit to the Guinness Storehouse, where the perfect pint is served at the required 6 degrees Celsius, is a must on a visit to Dublin.

2. The Confession Box

88 Marlborough Street, Dublin 1, 01 8747339, www.facebook.com/pages/category/Pub/The-Confession-Box-769555249806169/

This quiet and unassuming pub acquired its colourful name for the role it played in the Irish War of Independence (1919–1921). During

the bitter conflict the Catholic Church took issue with some of the leaders' penchant for violence and had them excommunicated, with Bishop Daniel Cohalan of Cork at the forefront of issuing the decrees. It was rumoured that many of those who were told to leave the Church, including the leader of the insurgents, Cork native Michael Collins, would drop into what was then the Maid of Erin pub to receive communion and have their confessions heard by sympathetic priests taking respite from their duties at the nearby Pro-Cathedral. Thus this pub acquired its name. The size of the premises, compared to the impressively huge church down the road, makes the name even more appropriate. Like so many other Dublin drinking establishments, the Confession Box reinforces its history with many visual reminders; there are a considerable number of Michael Collins photographs scattered through the premises.

Located at 88 Marlborough Street, on the bottom floor at the side of the now closed, and much lamented, Boyer's department store of North Earl Street, this pub is part of an impressive Edwardian building. Here, according to the pub's website, you are 'guaranteed a good pint and no penance'. Listeners of the Dublin radio station 98 FM certainly agreed, as they voted it 'Best Pint of Guinness in Dublin' in 2014 and 2015 – an accolade as highly sought as total absolution by many.

The pub also has an older, if lesser known, claim to fame. Diony-
sius Lardner, a notable scientist, economist and editor of *Cabinet
Cyclopedia* – a self-improvement 'Family Library' published between
1829 and 1846, containing 61 titles in 133 volumes – was born here
in 1793. The prospectus released with the books was in keeping with
the times: 'Nothing will be admitted into the pages of the 'CABINET
CYCLOPAEDIA' which can have the most remote tendency to offend
public or private morals. To enforce the cultivation of religion and
the practice of virtue should be a principal object with all who under-
take to inform the public mind.'

Later the pub was acquired by Michael O'Flanagan, who renamed
it O'Flanagan's, the name under which it traded until 1965. O'Flanagan and his brother, Kevin, were famous athletes, and are the only
set of brothers to have represented Ireland at both soccer and rugby
at senior level, a feat never likely to be repeated.

The story and circumstances surrounding their famous achievement are quite remarkable. Michael was a member of the famous
team that won the rugby Grand Slam in 1948 by beating England,
Wales and Scotland. He also played for Dublin soccer club Bohemians, and won his only cap for the Irish national team as a late
call-up in 1946. His brother Kevin, a former national sprint champion
and qualified doctor, had moved to London in 1945 and became a
member of Arsenal football club, where he was known as the 'Flying
Doc' to the Highbury supporters. While in London, Kevin O'Flanagan also played for the London Irish rugby union team.

The Ireland–England soccer game held in Dublin in 1946 holds
historical significance. Ireland's official football association had
been partitioned just weeks before the formation of the Irish Free
State in 1921, when London had sided with Belfast in an attempt to
bring members from the south back on board. In September 1946
the English Football Association unexpectedly accepted an invitation
from their Irish compatriots to send a team to Dublin. The Taoiseach, Éamon de Valera, a controversial figure in Britain because of
Ireland's neutrality in the recent war, honoured the English when
he hosted the first ever official pre-match lunch reception for a
visiting team. It was a welcome meal because it was a time of harsh
rationing in Britain. The English goalkeeper, Frank Swift, who later

died in the Munich air disaster which claimed the lives of many of the Manchester United football team, wrote in his autobiography of the 'sheer joy of sitting down to a five-course meal in Dublin's swanky Gresham Hotel'.

Kevin O'Flanagan was working in Saint Mary's Hospital, Paddington, and after finishing the night shift he got an early morning flight to Dublin for the match. His brother Michael was in the family pub when he got a telephone call from the FAI to replace Dave Walsh from West Bromwich Albion, who had failed a late fitness test. Michael closed the pub, cycled five miles to his house in Terenure to collect his football boots, and proceeded to Dalymount Park in Phibsboro for the match. It was only in the dressing room that the brothers realised they would both be playing on the Irish team that day. Despite their best efforts, the Irish team was beaten 1–0 in front of a crowd of 42,000 people. In 1947 Kevin O'Flanagan was capped by the Irish rugby team in a match against Australia. He died in 2006, while his brother Michael passed away on 12 September 2015 at the age of 92.

Such was the strength of sporting connections with the pub that a group of sports journalists who were in for a pint one night in 1961 decided it was the perfect place to found the Soccer Writers' Association of Ireland (SWAI).

Inside the Confession Box is a very small pub, barely larger than the size of the average Irish living room. The lighting is dim and the walls are covered with pictures of old Dublin, along with those of Irish revolutionaries. Traditional Irish music is frequent, and is aimed more at the local market, making this establishment an attractive option for those looking for some of the best aspects of a Dublin city pub without the sometimes madding crowds brought by tourism.

The Irish War of Independence

The Irish War of Independence was a guerrilla conflict between the British state and its forces in Ireland, and Irish republican guerrillas in the Irish Republican Army. The war ran between 1919 and 1921, but violence preceded these dates and continued afterwards. A political confrontation between the separatist Sinn Féin party, who after winning the general election of 1918 declared an Irish Republic, and the British administration based in Dublin Castle, occurred concurrently to the ongoing armed conflict. A third strand of the conflict lay in the northern province of Ulster, which was majority Unionist – or pro-British – and opposed Sinn Féin. This led to violence between the Protestant Unionists and the mainly Catholic Irish nationalist minority there. The conflict produced in the region of 2,500 deaths, although this has proven difficult to authenticate. The War of Independence ended with the signing of the Anglo-Irish Treaty in December 1921, which created two separate autonomous dominions within the British Empire – the Irish Free State and Northern Ireland, comprising six of the nine counties of Ulster. The Irish Free State, following a brief civil war between pro- and anti-Treaty sides, moved towards full independence from Britain with the adoption of a new constitution in 1937 and the declaration of a republic in 1949. Northern Ireland remains a constituent country of the United Kingdom.

3. The Hacienda

15 Mary Street Little, Dublin 1, 01 8730535, www.facebook.com/ Hacienda-Bar-Dublin-116745118384871/

This is an unusual pub in a city and country renowned for its open door policy when it comes to drinking establishments. To gain admittance the potential customer has to ring a bell and pass muster with the door staff before partaking of the delights within. It is not possible to see from the outside what those delights might be, as the windows are set high up on the stucco-covered walls in the style of – you may have guessed this – a Spanish hacienda. With its red tiles coming a third of the way down the front wall, like an untidy fringe, the charm of the building may not be obvious at first. Some might consider it a gimmick and an attention-seeking device, but there is no doubt that it has caught the imagination of many people. Hollywood actor Matthew McConaughey has been here in

the past. Once inside, the visitor can thrill at the eclectic hodgepodge that is the décor or partake in a game of pool. Located right beside the city's Victorian fruit and vegetable market, in a decidedly non-Mediterranean climate, and a less than attractive streetscape, this Spanish villa may be an oddity and a curiosity, but it adds another tone to the ever-widening palette of the Dublin bar scene. It only opens at 8 p.m., so the visitor can get a siesta in beforehand. Much of the charm of this pub is embodied in the eccentric owner, Shay. Those who frequent this establishment swear by it being the coolest thing since the Big Bang, and gush about the collegiality of its denizens. There is only one way to find out: ring the bell.

Matt Talbot and the 'Demon Drink'

One man who did his best to cut down alcohol sales figures in Dublin pubs was Matt Talbot. Ireland loves her martyrs, and one of the most revered of them all is the 'Venerable' Matt Talbot. His was a difficult upbringing, and Talbot suffered the worst privations of tenement life. He started working for Burke's Wine Merchants in Dublin at the age of twelve, where he acquired a taste for alcohol, often arriving home drunk. His father worked in the Customs House near Dublin Port, as the manager of the bonded spirits section. Thinking he would be able to keep a closer eye on his son he secured the young Matt a job there, but this only brought Talbot closer to temptation and his dissolution continued apace. At his lowest point Matt Talbot stole a fiddle from a blind musician on the street and sold it to buy drink. After a prolonged period of alcoholism, which left him an indigent beggar, he decided to take the pledge, an oath swearing off alcohol designed by temperance campaigner Father Matthews in conjunction with the Catholic Church. To atone for his past indiscretions Talbot slept on boards on an iron bedstead in his mother's room, using only a block of wood as a pillow. He only slept three-and-a-half hours each night, clutching a statue of the Virgin Mary. He ate stale bread and drank cold tea, allowing himself some meat at Christmas time, and took to wearing chains and cords under his clothes to indicate his desire to live a slave of the Virgin Mary. These were not discovered until he was brought to Jervis Street Hospital following a heart attack. Matt Talbott is not officially a saint, but his asceticism and self-mortification have made him a figure of worship for many Catholic alcoholics in Ireland and North America in particular. There is a small statue in memory of Matt Talbot at the spot where he died on Granby Lane.

4. Jack Nealon's

165-166 Capel Street, Dublin 1, 01 8723247,
www.facebook.com/jacknealonspub

When it was announced that Jack Nealon's was due to close in April 2017, after over 100 years in operation on gritty Capel Street, there was widespread wailing and gnashing of teeth. The shocking news was brought to the world by barrister Colm O'Byrne in a tweet: 'Terrible news. Lovely Nealon's Bar on Capel St is to close down in April. Vulture fund. All staff laid off.' Thankfully, financial restructuring of some arcane type has allowed this exceptionally well-preserved Georgian building to continue trading. The 200-year-old gold gilded ceiling is considered to be one of the best examples of ornate plasterwork extant in the capital city. Combined with the open fire, dark booths, brass fittings and subtle lighting, the word 'cosy' could have been invented for Nealon's. The second floor is home to an excellent cocktail lounge and boasts a wide selection of spirits, almost as wide as the selection of people who pass through the front doors. Popular with the LGBT community, legal eagles from the nearby Four Courts, live music fans, and numerous other hard-to-define elements, this is the type of establishment that makes traditional Dublin pubs so unique on the world stage. As well as accommodating blues dance groups and poetry readings, it must be one of the few pubs in the world that plays host to meetings of a canary breeders' association. Rejoice that it still survives.

Kips

A 'kip', in old Dublin, was a mixture of a brothel and shebeen (an illegal drinking establishment) that sold whiskey or gin from tea cups till the early morning. If the enthusiastic punter wanted to keep on drinking after the bona fide pubs closed he could travel back into the city and visit one of the infamous kips around Capel Street or Parnell Square. One of the most famous was the Cafe Continental on Bolton Street, which operated from the 1930s to the mid-1960s, and was run by the inimitable 'Dolly' Fawcett. Sarah Anne (Dolly) Fawcett, originally from Wicklow, married John Albert Hutchinson, a man who was rumoured to have been a former Dublin Metropolitan Police officer before he lost his job because of his association with the notorious cafe. From the outside the Cafe Continental was an innocent late-night cafe, but those who frequented it often consumed whiskey in their coffee, while Dolly served up 'red biddy' (a mixture of red wine and methanol), poitín and watered-down whiskey. The Continental was also a popular place for prostitutes to find clients. In Dublin slang an ugly woman is still sometimes referred to as one of 'Dolly Fawcett's chambermaids'. Other kips included Toni's Cafe on 23 Harcourt Road – which became the Manhattan Cafe in the early 1950s, a favourite for taxi drivers, musicians and students, until its closure in the early 2000s.

The notorious Catacombs in the basement of 13 Fitzwilliam Place was another popular after-hours drinking establishment and flop-house in the late 1940s for Dublin's bohemian set. The old Georgian pile, a labyrinth of cellars and pantries, was opened as an 'underground' club by Englishman Richard 'Dickie' Wymann, a one-time cruise liner cocktail shaker and former London nightclub manager who moved to Dublin following the death of his British Army officer boyfriend in the Second World War. After McDaid's pub closed, Dublin's artistic and literary set would head to the Catacombs and drink until the early morning. Regulars included writers Brendan Behan, Patrick Kavanagh, J.P. Donleavy, Anthony Cronin and Flann O'Brien. Behan famously recalled that it was a place where 'men had women, men had men and women had women'.

5. Madigan's

25 North Earl Street, Dublin 1, 01 8740646, www.madigansearlst.com

In 1932 the *Irish Times* lashed out against cocktails: 'The cocktail fulfils no useful function, it is supposed by the many to induce an appetite and stimulate intelligent conversation; in fact it absorbs the pancreatic juices and encourages cheap wit.' Later in 1937 the same paper reported the belief of a doctor from Clare Mental Hospital: 'Now that women have taken with avidity to tobacco and cocktails, one can visualise the most appalling results for the human race at a not far distant date.'

The owners of Madigan's of North Earl Street were obviously not influenced by this conservative concept, and offered an extensive range of cocktails to the discerning customer in the early 1960s. Five shillings purchased a Singapore Sling, an Alexander or Frank's Special; Gin Slings, Moscow Mules and High Balls were available for a shilling less. The bright orange menu did not provide the customer with a breakdown of the ingredients, but the front cover was interesting. It featured a pencil drawing of Nelson's Pillar – a statue of Lord Horatio Nelson on O'Connell Street, later blown up by Irish republicans in 1966 – with a cartoon bubble emanating from his mouth containing the words 'for a topping cocktail'. The bar has outlived the statue – Madigan's is still open for business.

Nelson's Pillar is a vivid part of Irish social and cultural history. The granite structure was partially destroyed by a bomb planted by Irish republican terrorists in 1966 in the curiously named 'Operation Humpty Dumpty'. After some limited protest the destruction job was subsequently finished off by the Irish army. In 2003 it was replaced by the Spire of Dublin, designed by Ian Ritchie.

North Earl Street was named by Henry Moore, the Third Viscount Moore and the First Earl of Drogheda, after himself. The earl was responsible for laying out the streets in this area of Dublin after the Restoration of the monarchy in 1660; he also saw fit to name the nearby Henry and Moore streets in his own honour.

This beautiful pub, established in 1922, contains some fantastic features, including priceless stained glass windows by Harry Clarke, widely regarded as the best Irish artist to ever work in the medium. Madigan's is not a pub that shouts out loud. It is a great place for a quiet drink in the middle of this frenetic part of Dublin city centre. For those who like plain and simple food there is a no-frills carvery on the premises.

Smoking Ban

In March 2004 Ireland became the first country in the world to introduce legislation banning smoking in workplaces, including pubs. Publicans threatened to challenge the legislation, claiming they did not have sufficient time to make adjustments to buildings to incorporate smoking areas. In fairness, it did prove a difficult task, particularly for those land-locked pubs in towns and cities where there was no room to build outdoor areas. Many of the oldest pubs were the worst affected in this regard. Notwithstanding the concerns of many publicans, the ban was enforced from 29 March and resulted in substantial changes in the layout of many pubs. Beer gardens and heated patios proliferated. 'Smirting' – a combination of smoking and flirting – became a new social phenomenon. The ban was perceived as a huge success by health authorities. Cigarette sales fell by 60 per cent in bars, and it was reported that 7,000 people gave up smoking in the first twelve months after the ban came into effect. However, not all publicans were happy. Within months, pub owners reported a 25 per cent drop in sales, with rural pubs being worst hit, and many called for the ban to be eased. However, popular sentiment was not in agreement and, after some initial teething problems, the ban ultimately proved a winner, with a number of other countries following suit. These days research indicates that most customers, and even many smokers, are happy to drink in a non-smoking environment. In retrospect, it was a storm in a teacup.

6. The Oval

78 Middle Abbey Street, Dublin 1, 01 8721264, www.theovalbar.com

With its original Victorian exterior, including the unusual 'lunette' oval window, this pub is a haven of tranquillity in the busy city centre. It was not always so. Easter Monday, 24 April 1916 seemed a day like any other at the Oval, until the Irish Volunteers captured the nearby General Post Office (GPO) and proclaimed an Irish Republic.

In the years leading up to 1916 this pub had been popular with members of the Irish Citizen Army and the Irish Volunteers, who often dropped in after manoeuvres while waiting for nearby trams. The week that followed Easter Monday brought chaos, devastation, death and destruction, both to the city of Dublin and to the Oval. By Wednesday the HMS *Helga* had sailed up the Liffey and commenced shelling Liberty Hall and the GPO. At precisely 10 a.m. on Thursday 27 April, the fate of the Oval was sealed. Trajectories were set on the *Helga* and the GPO and surrounding buildings were all directly hit. Fires blazed in Sackville Street (now O'Connell Street) and Abbey Street; before long an inferno had engulfed the city centre. The Oval and surrounding buildings were destroyed. Abbey and Sackville Streets smouldered for days as ruin and rubble scattered the pavements.

The original Oval claims to have been established in 1822, making it the oldest surviving pub in the Abbey Street area. The pub was first owned by a James Cooney. By 1848 it had changed hands a number of times and was in possession of Bridget and Peter Coyle. This was a bleak time in Irish history; famine and emigration ravaged the country, although Dublin did not suffer the catastrophic loss of life that occurred in the west and south-west of the country. Peter Coyle was a coachbuilder and saw the pub as a good investment because the ticket office and starting point for journeys by Royal Mail coach to Enniskillen, Cavan, Sligo and Westport were located next door at Number 77. Coyle repaired coaches while his wife saw to the needs of the thirsty travellers. In 1902, the Oval was acquired by John J. Egan, who also owned a pub at 81–82 Talbot Street, allowing him to live in Glenageary, then, and now, one of the most fashionable suburbs on the south side of the city. After Egan purchased the premises he immediately closed it and created a lavish Edwardian restoration in keeping with the finer establishments at the time. After the reopening, the pub was a substantial beneficiary of the fourth estate as Independent Newspapers was, and is, located at Numbers 87–90.

All was well until the destruction wrought by the 1916 Rising, but John Egan was made of stern stuff and when the dust settled he set about rebuilding his business. When the Oval reopened in 1922 Egan had luck on his side. While many buildings in the vicinity were again destroyed during the Civil War, the Oval remained largely unscathed.

Egan spent exactly fifty years in the business before selling it on to James Browne in 1964. Thirty years later it was acquired by Charlie Chawke, who added it to his burgeoning empire of Dublin pubs. The Oval is a perfect stop in the middle of a hectic shopping spree in the nearby Henry Street area. That it played such a central role in the fight for Irish freedom is an additional feather in its cap and a further reason to sample a top-class pint of Guinness in this most convenient of locations.

7. Pantibar

7-8 Capel Street, Dublin 1, 01 8740710, www.pantibar.com

Rory O'Neill – better known by his stage name Panti Bliss – and his Pantibar have been at the centre of the LGBTI scene in Ireland since its establishment in 2007. He runs it with his business partner, restaurateur Jay Burke. O'Neill, originally from Ballinrobe, County Mayo, is an iconic character in contemporary Ireland. His alter ego, Panti, is Ireland's best known drag queen and the public face of

Dublin Pride each year. From 1996 to 2012 Panti hosted the hugely popular Alternative Miss Ireland pageant, and for many years ran a weekly karaoke show called the Casting Couch at the Front Lounge pub. Rory's full stage name is 'Pandora Panti Bliss' and his colourful career has included dancing on stage with American singing star Cyndi Lauper in Japan during her 1994 Twelve Deadly Cyns Tour.

'Pantigate'

On 11 January 2014 Rory O'Neill appeared on RTÉ's *The Saturday Night Show* with Brendan O'Connor where they discussed homophobia in Ireland. O'Neill alleged that some individuals involved in Irish journalism were homophobic. Those mentioned threatened RTÉ and O'Neill with legal action. RTÉ subsequently removed that section of the interview from their online archive. On 25 January O'Connor issued a public apology on behalf of RTÉ, which paid €85,000 to those named by O'Neill. The issue was later discussed by the Irish government and in the European Parliament. Irish MEP Paul Murphy called the payments 'a real attack on the freedom of speech'. RTÉ's head of television later defended the €85,000 payments stating that they saved RTÉ 'an absolute multiple' in the long term.

On 1 February 2014, O'Neill – performing as Panti – gave a 'Noble Call' speech at the Abbey Theatre in response to the events surrounding the RTÉ controversy. The speech was described as 'the most eloquent Irish speech' in almost 200 years by *Irish Times* journalist Fintan O'Toole and was widely praised across the world, garnering over 200,000 views in just two days.

In 2015 a documentary film about Rory called *The Queen of Ireland* was released to widespread critical claim. The Conor Hogan-directed work foregrounded O'Neil's central role in the campaign for equal marriage rights. One of the seminal scenes in the film shows Rory – in full drag – walking through his hometown of Ballinrobe with his mother, Fin, and father, Rory Senior. In many ways it was a triumphant day for Ireland. Only seven days earlier the country had voted yes in the referendum on marriage equality.

In June 2018 a brick was thrown through the window of Pantibar by a teenage boy on the eve of Dublin Gay Pride. In inimitable style, Rory posted a photograph of the brick on Twitter alongside an attached note in Irish, which read: 'Piteoga amach as Eireann'. Beside the photograph, O'Neill wrote: 'A brick thrown through Pantibar's window just now. No one hurt. It says in Irish "FAIRIES (fags) OUT OF IRELAND". But we are Ireland.'

8. The Piper's Corner

105-106 Marlborough Street, Dublin 1, 01 8733503,
www.piperscorner.ie

One of the newest kids on the block on the Dublin pub scene, the Piper's Corner was opened in July 2017 by Seán Óg Potts, son of the famous uilleann piper Seán Potts, and long-time publican Eamonn Briody. This pub is right at the very heart of Dublin city, less than two minutes' walk from O'Connell Bridge and the city's main thoroughfare, and has quickly become a destination for fans of top-notch traditional Irish music. On the corner of Marlborough Street, this premises was formerly known as Seán O'Casey's, but will not be mistaken for anything other than its new name given the huge mural of renowned piper Seamus Ennis on the outside wall. Ennis, born in Finglas in Dublin in 1919, was famous for performing and collecting traditional Irish pipe music. He spent five years travelling the highroads and byways of Ireland collecting music and song for the Irish Folklore Commission between 1942 and 1947, and later helped to found Na Píobairí Uilleann (the Irish Pipers' Association), nurturing the talent of future generations of Irish musicians before his death in 1982.

Seán Potts is a well-known figure in Irish and Dublin Gaelic games, and this pub will definitely be on the trail of supporters of hurling and Gaelic football as it is none too far from Croke Park, the head-quarters and national stadium of the Gaelic Athletic Association. The

combination of top-class sport and music is sure to remain a definite winner for many years to come.

The Long Story of Good Friday

In 2010 a Limerick court case threw an international spotlight on Ireland's Good Friday alcohol legislation. The Celtic League Rugby Union scheduled a match between Munster and Leinster at Thomond Park in Limerick for 2 April – Good Friday. Vintners were up in arms. They estimated €10 million in turnover would go a-begging. After a court case appealing for a lifting of the law, widely dubbed 'The Good Friday Disagreement', the publicans were successful and for the first time since 1927 people were allowed to consume alcohol in ordinary licensed premises in Ireland on the holy day. Surprisingly, this temporary legislation did not result in a relaxation of the law; it was a once-off derogation. The case highlighted divergent viewpoints in Irish society. Brother Seán O'Connor, head of the Franciscan Friary in Moyross, Limerick, a group lauded for their work in a severely disadvantaged community, took a dim view of the legal decision: 'I heard someone quoted this week who said that rugby is more important than religion – that's just ridiculous and it's a shame. If you identify yourself as a Catholic then you should be nowhere near Thomond Park or a pub on that day … this is like something out of the Old Testament. If you're going against God and making a public stand about it then you are serving Mammon over God. I don't care how much money you pull in, it will backfire on you on a spiritual level.' Politicians of various hues exercised their verbal dexterity. Independent Senator Joe O'Toole wanted the law changed: 'Everyone's a winner. Free will prevails; the Church–State separation is maintained. We render to Munster the things that are Munster's and to God the things that are God's. We save jobs. The economy gains.' Senator Donie Cassidy, Fianna Fáil stalwart, regretted the lack of respect for 'the crucifixion of the Good Lord.' On 25 March 2010, Judge Tom O'Donnell, while recognising the potential for 'controversy in several quarters', granted Limerick publicans an exemption from the state ban on opening on Good Friday. Because the stadium was allowed to serve alcohol it would have been absurd, he contended, not to let pubs in the vicinity trade. Publicans in Limerick were granted legal permission to trade between 6 p.m. and 11.30 p.m. In January 2018 the ban on Good Friday closing was finally lifted, and publicans threw open their doors on the holy day that year for the first time since 1927.

9. Ryan's of Parkgate Street

28 Parkgate Street, Arran Quay, Dublin 8, 01 6776097,
www.fxbuckley.ie/ryans-victorian-pub

A stone's throw from the city's largest train station and largest urban green space, Ryan's pub, established in 1886, is a work of high Victorian art. For those availing of transportation at nearby Heuston Station, it is a perfect chance to sample the atmosphere of

a beautiful Dublin city pub steeped in history, while a walk in the nearby Phoenix Park, home of the National Zoological Gardens, is a perfect way to build up a thirst for this rarefied drinking establishment. The interior is full of ornate detail, including two beautiful snugs, the oldest two-faced clock in Ireland, gorgeous gas lamps, antique whiskey barrels, and an old booth where the original owner, Bongo Ryan, sat and observed proceedings in the bar. The impressive clock was manufactured by the Frengly Brothers German Clock Company in the late 1800s, and built into the pub in 1886. Like many pub clocks, it is set five minutes fast – in this case by Mungo Ryan, ostensibly so that none of his patrons would miss their train from the nearby station. The metal grates integrated into the wood around the bar for clients to light their cigarettes, cigars and pipes are a rare feature.

Ryan's is one of the best preserved of all the remaining Victorian pubs in Dublin with a wealth of detail that must almost qualify it as a museum.

It was nearly destroyed in the early years of the twentieth century when Mungo Ryan briefly considered modernising the pub. Luckily, before proceeding, he consulted with the owner of the equally beautiful Palace Bar in Fleet Street, and both agreed they would keep their premises in the Victorian style.

One of the more unique features of the pub is the sheer volume of greenery, including the multiple hanging baskets from the roof – unlikely to have been there during the Victorian era, but a beautiful sight nonetheless. In 2006 it was bought by the prominent butcher chain F.X. Buckley, which has turned it into a high-end gastropub experience. It is one not to be missed for the visitor to this part of the city.

When the Pubs Saved the Economy

In 1970 Irish bank workers went on a national strike for six months in pursuit of better pay and conditions. At a time when ATMs were only a distant dream there was a genuine concern the economy would run short of available cash. Into the breach stepped the pubs of the nation, which cashed workers' cheques and kept the financial wheels of the country oiled. It was a striking indication of the centrality of the pub to Irish social and cultural life. While there was a small element of fraud, the system worked well enough until the banks and their staff finally came to an accommodation. By the end of the strike, people were even creating their own chequebooks, as the originals were no longer available. It is a great story to tell in the pub.

10. Slattery's of Capel Street

129 Capel Street, Dublin 1, 01 8746844, www.slatterys.bar

Slattery's on Capel Street is one of the last remaining early houses in Dublin, opening at 7 a.m. on weekdays and 10.30 a.m. on Sundays. It is also the only remaining Victorian-built early opening pub. For both those reasons it is worth being on the itinerary of a tour of the pubs of Ireland's capital city. While some early houses have a less than a salubrious reputation, and might be best left off the tourist's pub itinerary, Slattery's offers a more rarefied experience, including full breakfast from opening. Looking at the state-of-the-art decor it is hard to believe that only a few short years ago this was a grungy rock-music-orientated pub. There is also a commemorative wall in honour of those who fought and died during the 1916 Rising, which includes an impressive collection of uniforms, medals, documents and weaponry from the time. Like Capel Street itself, this

establishment is an energetic melting pot of a place. For the pub completest it would be a shame not to include this fine establishment on your bucket list.

Early Houses

From 1927 early house pubs were allowed to open at 7.30 a.m. in Ireland. Originally created to serve dock workers, market traders, milkmen, bakers and others who were up to work early in the morning, there are roughly fifteen remaining early house licences in Dublin, with none granted since 1962. In 2008 plans were made to abolish them but, after protracted political discussion, the legislation remains on the statute books. There are approximately 50 live early house licences left in Ireland, but anecdotal evidence suggests many of them are only used occasionally, some not at all. In general, early houses are not interested in all-night revellers and most are very selective on whom they let in. The now-defunct satirical *The Slate* magazine ran an interesting article on Dublin early houses in 2003. The first rule of early houses, it said, is 'never talk to anyone with a plastic bag on the table in the front of them. This could contain a gun, some heroin, a dead baby or their soiled underpants – none of which you want to engage with at that stage of a night out.' Neither should you try to put on a Dublin accent because 'you will have your head kicked in if you pretend to be a local while talking about the oneness of life and gurning your head off.' Should you insist on including some on your Dublin pub quest do not say you have not been warned. In truth, most early houses are quiet establishments where you will be left to your own devices.

Dublin City South Suburbs

1. The Dropping Well

Classon's Bridge, Milltown, Dublin 6, 01 4973969,
www.droppingwell.com

Since it was first established in 1847, the Dropping Well has had eight owners and is now under the stewardship of serial publican Charlie Chawke. It was first licensed as a community morgue and pub after John Howe and his wife approached the authorities offering to set up a facility to help deal with the horrendous effects of the Great Famine, which caused a constant flow of dead bodies coming down the nearby Dodder River. In his valiant efforts to help alleviate the appalling situation Howe contracted an infection and died in 1850. His wife continued the business until 1855 before passing it on to a relative recorded only as Miss Williams. In 1908 the premises were acquired by P.H. Meagher, a keen sports enthusiast, who completed a lavish upgrade, including the installation of a boxing ring in the premises, in which he would take on all comers. The front of the establishment is now called 'The Boxer Lounge' in his honour.

The Dropping Well is located on the site of a former mill owned by John Classon, after whom the nearby Classon's Bridge is named. Like many of the smaller river crossings in the city, Classon's Bridge was destroyed in 1921 during the Irish War of Independence, after a number of attempts to bring it down. It was subsequently repaired in 1928 when the original structure was widened and a new bridge built on top of the remaining parts of the original. A small distance upstream from the bridge there is the unique sight of a statue of a rhino in the middle of the river.

The pub got its name from a nearby underground well which flooded every winter and spring; before that it was known as Classon's Bridge House. For over 40 years the pub was a stop on the Dartry tramline, which served the premises every half hour. It is now just a few seconds from the Milltown Luas stop and is close to the 128, 44 and 48A bus routes, so there is no excuse for not taking a trip out this way.

Bona Fide Pubs

Bona fide public houses utilised a legal loophole – a hangover from coaching days – which allowed a genuine traveller to partake of alcohol outside normal hours, provided he was three miles away from his normal place of residence. In Dublin city the limit extended to five miles from a habitual residence. The customer had to have 'travelled in good faith', not for the purposes of taking refreshment, but could go into an inn for 'refreshment in the course of a journey, whether of business or pleasure'. It was a contentious area. The court had to prove the publican did not believe his customer was a bona fide traveller when serving outside normal hours. It was said some creative drinkers would send a letter to themselves using the address of a friend who lived the required distance away from their desired pub. They could then show the letter to the publican to pacify him. Famous Dublin bona fide pubs included Lamb Doyle's in the foothills of the Dublin Mountains, the Deadman's Inn in Lucan, the Igo Inn in Ballybrack, Walsh's Sandyford House (then known as the Widow Flavin's), and the Dropping Well in Dartry.

Drinkers in the city centre drove out to the suburbs and vice versa. Flann O'Brien famously observed that 'he drove himself to drink'. The law was finally changed in 1943 whereby bona fide travellers could no longer be served between midnight and 6 a.m. Bona fide pubs were eventually abolished in 1963. The widespread use of cars brought the curtains down on a unique phase of Irish pub and social history.

2. The Oarsman

8-10 Bridge Street, Ringsend, Dublin 4, 01 6689360,
www.theoarsman.ie

In architectural terms the façade of this pub is of considerable note. The elaborate stucco work on the pediment, featuring a representation of a round tower, a Celtic high cross and an Irish wolfhound, was completed by Burnet and Comerford, whose masterpiece was the sadly demolished Irish House bar on Winetavern Street and Wood Quay. Adding further historical currency to this establishment is its inclusion in *Ulysses*, albeit as Tulley's pub. Inside, the vaulted ceiling, bar counter and barrel taps are in situ since 1816. The full-length, gold-trim mirror and eclectic mix of rugby and maritime memorabilia add to the décor. This pub is only a short distance from the 3 Arena, Bord Gáis Energy Theatre and the Aviva Stadium. The extensive Grand Canal Dock development is also only a stone's throw away – all of which makes for a diverse clientele. The hipster will have no problem here as they stock a diverse and rotating array of craft beers.

'Gastropubs'

It might not be a universally favoured term, but at least the origin of 'gastropub' is clear. It was first used by David Eyre and Mike Belben in 1991 when they took over the Eagle Pub in Clerkenwell, London in 1991. The *Collins Dictionary* does not mince its words: it describes a gastropub as 'one that serves very good food'. Perhaps Heston Blumenthal is as good an authority as exists: 'The food should be populist, robustly flavoured and it should go well with beer. There should also be proper space, rather than a few tokenistic bar stools, for people who just want to drink, and, perhaps, get drunk.'

3. The Old Spot

14 Bath Avenue, Sandymount, Dublin 4, 01 6605599,
www.theoldspot.ie

The Old Spot is at the very top of the gastropub tree. It is one of only two pubs in Dublin to make the *Michelin Eating Out in Pubs Guide* three years running (2016-2018); the other is the nearby Chophouse. With its distressed wooden floors, exposed wooden beams, and red-bricked dining room with vintage maps of New York City and ink drawings of University of Dublin (i.e. Trinity College) sporting encounters from the 1800s, the interior is nothing if not eclectic.

The Old Spot was opened in September 2014 by brothers Paul and Barry McNerney in the former Lansdowne Bar. They had found previous success with the nearby Juniors Deli & Cafe, established in 2008. Two years later the dynamic duo added Paulie's Pizza and Barry's Bar. For the Old Spot they joined forces with Stephen Cooney and Brian O'Malley of the Bath Pub. Head chef Fiachra Kenny, who had spent time in the kitchens of Forest Avenue, Pichet and the Green Hen, has placed a strong emphasis on full Irish flavours from the start. This pub is highly rated for its food and has garnered a number of awards during its short existence, including four consecutive entries in the Michelin Guide under the heading of 'Eating Out in Dublin' – one of only two Dublin pubs to hold such an honour. It is particularly praised for its extensive wine menu and the quality of its cocktails.

4. Royal Oak, Kilmainham

11 Kilmainham Lane, Dublin 8, 01 6713967,
www.facebook.com/theoakd8

'The Royal Oak' is a common pub name in Great Britain, commemorating an escapade where King Charles II escaped from Cromwellian soldiers by climbing up into an oak tree in Boscobel, near Wolverhampton, in 1651. Despite some of the Roundheads – as Cromwell's uncompromising soldiers were called – passing directly under the tree, the king remained undetected, and the British monarchy was eventually restored in 1660.

This Royal Oak pub is as near to a typical Irish hostelry in a country town as it is possible to get in the city of Dublin. Only a few minutes away from the Irish Museum of Modern Art (IMMA) and Kilmainham Gaol, this unique venue is rated as one of the best in the city by many seasoned bar hounds. It is very small – there are only two tables and a forest of stools – but what it lacks in size it certainly makes up for in character. Opened in 1845 to serve the patrons and staff of what was then the Royal Hospital (now the IMMA) the pebble-dashed exterior appears to have had very little alteration since those distant days. The Garda station immediately across the road from the pub was once an entrance point to the hospital, the oldest classical building in Ireland. The Royal Hospital, built in 1680, was modelled on Les Invalides in Paris. Originally designed to house 400 army pensioners, it held up to 2,500 over the course of its life. In 1922 it was handed over to the Irish Free State; five years later the last remaining pensioner departed to its sister hospital, Chelsea in London. From 1930 to 1950 it served as the headquarters of the Gardaí, the Irish national police force. After falling into considerable disrepair, Taoiseach (Prime Minister) Charles Haughey gave the go-ahead for a £3 million four-year restoration project in 1987 – the same length of time it took to construct the original building. The gardens, once used for their health-restoring properties by the residents, and subsequently as the private gardens of the master of the hospital (the then head of the British Army in Ireland), were also part of the extensive refurbishment. In 1991 the 48-acre site became home to the IMMA.

Inside, the decor of the Royal Oak pub may be stuck firmly in the mid-1970s, but it has found favour with Thom Yorke of Radiohead, among other notables. There are very few one-room pubs left in Ireland – let alone the capital city – so this one should feature highly on any visitor's list. Rugby appears to be a sport of choice here, if the framed British and Irish Lions and Munster shirts are anything to go by. There is no excuse for not getting here, as there is a Dublin bike station a few minutes away. Under the ownership of the Costello family since 1972, this is a great pub with a proud reputation for accepting all-comers.

5. Slattery's of Rathmines

217–219 Lower Rathmines Road, Dublin 6, 01 4972052, www. facebook.com/pages/category/Pub/Mb-Slatterys-1020953627988891

M.B. Slattery's is a lot of things for a lot of people. Rathmines has traditionally been a part of Dublin where those from the countryside found their first rental accommodation, and for whom Slattery's was one of the first urban hostelries of choice. Strike up a conversation with a rural Irish dweller who has spent some time residing in the capital city and chances are they will have fond memories of this storied pub. At least that was the way in the past. Increasing gentrification has restricted the rental market in Dublin, and pushed many who would like to live in the area further afield, but it is still a great mixed urban area looked over by the local Catholic church and the clock tower of the impressive town hall. Rathmines really is a proper urban village. It has a lively main street, complete with a shopping centre and cinema complex, post office, library, schools and a third-level college. At the foundation of the Irish state Rathmines was a desirable address: Seán O'Casey had a memorable character called 'the Lady from Rathmines' in his play *The Plough and the Stars*. The upper-class woman got lost in the city centre during the Easter Rising, as her travels had never previously taken her to the undesirable city-centre tenements in which the other characters live. After being taken over by Dublin Corporation in 1930 the once predominantly Protestant, and Unionist, area of Rathmines gradually declined, with much of the fine Victorian housing stock being subdivided into bedsits. Even the beautiful town hall, designed by Sir Thomas Drew in 1895, was subdivided into classrooms for use by the College of Commerce. Times have moved on, and things have changed, but this pub is still like Rathmines itself – an eclectic and ever-changing locale.

Having been under a number of different ownerships since its establishment in 1844, it was in 1953 that Martin B. Slattery put his name above the door here after he paid the then princely sum of £10,250 for the pub.

Upstairs in Slattery's provides a moveable feast of musical genres, something to suit all tastes will eventually appear on the schedule. With its tongue-and-groove wooden ceilings, creaking floors and great snug, this is a genuine Irish pub with none of the pretension of many newer bars. The red leatherette couches sag in the middle, and many of the tables are wonky, but the pint of Guinness and the bar staff are top drawer. This is the type of establishment that will hopefully always hold a place in the heart of Irish people, operating, as it does, as a bridge between rural and urban.

The Day Formerly Known as Arthur's Day

Arthur's Day was established, some would say invented, in 2009 by Diageo to commemorate the 250th anniversary of the founding of the Guinness brewing company. From the start there were rumblings of discontent. Despite endorsements from high-profile celebrities like humanitarian and musician Bob Geldof, film director Guy Richie, and former England footballer Peter Crouch, others, such as singer Christy Moore, and film director Lenny Abrahamson, criticised the venture. The US-based *Huffington Post* dubbed it 'Diageo Day' and called for a boycott. Critics pointed to the holding of the event on a Thursday night – the traditional student drinking night in the cities – as opportunist. The *Irish Times* termed it 'a master class in how to fabricate a national holiday' and referred to its 'a la carte attitude to traditional holidays'. It noted the countdown as a mimicking of the traditional welcome to the New Year, and the 'faux patriotism that comes with the celebration of a "national" drink' and what they termed the 'hagiographic treatment' of Arthur Guinness as a type of secular saint. It warned its readers: 'If Saint Patrick's Day, Christmas and Halloween are festivals that offer an excuse for drink, Diageo has flipped the concept on its head and made the drink an excuse for a festival.'

The mechanics of the day were straightforward. At 17.59 p.m. the brewing company asked drinkers to raise a toast to Arthur Guinness to celebrate the anniversary. There were various musical, social and cultural events run on the day throughout the city. Over the years the line-ups were stellar, and the day was celebrated across the globe. However, in 2012 there was widespread discontent when the Royal College of Physicians in Ireland reported a 30 per cent surge in ambulance call-outs on each successive Arthur's Day since its inception.

Finally things reached a head (pun intended) in 2013. In September a social media campaign called 'Boycott Arthur's Day' came to national and international attention. On 24 September a live debate was held on the current affairs television programme *Prime Time* on the national channel, RTE One.

It included a Guinness executive, Peter O'Brien, defending the celebration. The singer Christy Moore, a long-time critic and a recovering alcoholic, had released a single to mark the occasion which he sung live on the programme. After years of increasing discomfort among sections of the public the celebration came to an end and was replaced in 2014 by a short-lived programme to support emerging artists in Ireland called 'Guinness Amplify'. In September 2015 MSN News reported that a bar in Jundiaí, Brazil celebrated the occasion, while, nearer to the origin of the event, it was reported that Spell's Bar in Ballaghaderreen, County Roscommon celebrated 'The Day Formerly Known as Arthur's Day'. All in all, it is a great Irish story.

6. The Yellow House

1 Willbrook Road, Rathfarnham, Dublin 14, 01 4932994,
www.yellowhousepub.com

This iconic pub, particularly well known for its extensive food offering in recent times, is an impressive repository of social and cultural history. Like many origin stories concerning Irish and Dublin pubs, there are competing narratives. The original yellow house, after which the pub is named, may have been a thatched cottage on the present-day site of the nearby Church of the Annunciation. In 1798 the owner, Michael Eades, provided a safe house for members of the United Irishmen, who were in a position to overhear conversations among soldiers of the Rathfarnham Guard, stationed next door. In 1804, realising the subterfuge which had taken place, and that Eades himself was a member of the United Irishmen, the British authorities destroyed the building. In 1825 a new Yellow House arose from the ashes of the old and opened as a public house in 1827, under the stewardship of Mary Murray. The name may also have come from the unusual shade of bricks used in the construction of the building.

This area of Dublin is rich in history and the visitor could easily pass the day taking in the nearby delights of Rathfarnham Castle, Loreto Abbey, and Saint Enda's School. The latter was established by Irish freedom fighter Pádraig Pearse to educate young men through his nationalist-inspired curriculum and is today run as a museum in his honour. The original castle at Rathfarnham dates back to the Elizabethan period, and was built for Archbishop Adam Loftus, an ambitious Yorkshire clergyman who came to Ireland as chaplain to the Lord Deputy and quickly rose to become Archbishop of Dublin, Lord Chancellor of Ireland, and a founder of Trinity College. The castle, with its four flanker towers, is an excellent example of the fortified house in Ireland. In the late eighteenth century the house was remodelled, employing some of the finest architects of the day, including Sir William Chambers and James 'Athenian' Stuart.

The visitor is spoiled for green spaces with Marlay, Bushy and Dodder Parks all within easy walking distance. Rathfarnham is a genteel suburb and this is a suitably genteel establishment.

The highly regarded Morilles Bistro is on the second floor, an establishment highly regarded for its French-inspired cuisine and extensive wine list. All in all this building provides a pleasant experience for the genteel residents of this well-appointed Dublin suburb.

Dublin City North Suburbs

1. The Barber's

19 Lower Grangegorman Road, Dublin 7, 01 5394048,
www.thebarbers.ie

The running of an ancillary business in conjunction with a public house has a long, and not always noble, history in Ireland. A spirit grocer's licence allowed a publican to run a business of their choice along with dispensing alcohol. The Barber's might be the only pub in the history of Ireland where a customer can get their hair cut and have a drink at the same time. Then again, it may not, and that is the beauty of the Irish pub. It has been such a rich and diverse institution for so long that to prove or disprove this point would be well-nigh impossible. Whatever of that, there is a distinct pleasure in being able to make an online hair appointment knowing that when

you turn up you can have a drink near at hand; some might even consider it the pinnacle of civilisation. There is nothing bogus about this venture, as the owner, Chris Darby, is a barber and a former member of staff at Whelan's pub. The antique hairdryers used as lights and the barbers' chairs are beautiful objects indeed.

This is a pub of the new dispensation, in a part of the city that is undergoing rapid change. The Dublin Institute of Technology (newly renamed Technical University Dublin) is currently amalgamating its constituent schools on the nearby former grounds of Saint Brendan's Psychiatric Hospital, Grangegorman, and the social fabric of the area is changing fundamentally. It is likely this pub will prove a huge part of student life for many years to come. It is dog friendly, and holds regular women's social evenings, table quizzes, and an evolving roster of live music. This is a pub worth going out of the way for.

Licensed Vintners' Association

The Licensed Vintner's Association (LVA), the representative body of publicans in Dublin city and county and Bray, County Wicklow, claims to be the oldest trade association in the country, dating back to 1817, when it was founded as the Fair Trading Vintners' Society and Asylum. At its establishment, it had the twin aims of obtaining a fair deal on taxation from the British authorities and setting in place a system to help vintners and their families who had fallen on bad times. With the second aim they succeeded admirably by building a facility in Charlemont Street described as 'having a very commodious rear, comprising playground for the school, orchard and garden with a detached passage and gateway', as well as 'apartments for School Master and Mistress, [and] school rooms in which nearly one hundred children could be comfortably lodged'. The powerful body has sailed the ship of the Dublin pub through often choppy waters for 200 years, and represents some of the most successful businesspeople in the capital city. It has had a number of significant achievements over the years, including helping to block proposed cafe bar legislation in 2004. Under the able leadership of Donall O'Keefee, the LVA celebrated its 200th anniversary in lavish style in 2017. Eamon Casey, historian to the association, summed up the organisation's work: 'Their primary aims throughout the generations have remained consistent in that they seek only to run respectable, responsible and professional premises, be treated with justice and fairness by the legislators, to rear their families and be allowed to socially support and contribute to the broader community where they serve.' Publicans outside Dublin and Bray have a separate representative body, the Vintners' Federation of Ireland.

2. The Cobblestone

77 North King Street, Smithfield, Dublin 7, 01 8721799,
www.cobblestonepub.ie

The Cobblestone has a clever advertising slogan which draws its inspiration from the writer Brendan Behan, who infamously called himself 'a drinker with the writing problem'. The Cobblestone is 'a drinking pub with a music problem', and has been in the Mulligan family for five generations. The current owner, Tom, is a brother of famous uilleann piper Néillidh who, along with other members of Na Piobairí Uilleann, plays here on the first Tuesday night of every month. There is traditional Irish music here seven nights a week, and twice on Sundays. The pub is a brisk fifteen-minute walk from the city centre, and is served by the Luas, Dublin's light rail system. The tram stop is only a short walk across the beautiful cobbled plaza. This historic part of Dublin city has long been home to the fruit and vegetable wholesale market, and in recent years has become increasingly gentrified. It is now a very desirable place to live, and is home to the Old Jameson Whiskey Distillery and the Light House Cinema, as well as some nice cafes and restaurants. The area is also well known for its horse fair, which takes place on the first Sunday of March and September, and in recent years the plaza has housed an ice rink each Christmas. If traditional Irish music is on the wish list of the visitor to Dublin, this is a pub not to be missed.

Music Sessions in Irish Pubs

Traditional music sessions are central to Irish pub culture, and are a major tourist product in the country. The word 'session' – seisiún in Irish – simply means a group of people playing music together in either a private or public setting. In the past musicians played for pleasure but, with the advent of mass tourism, it has become a paid job for some. However, the traveller around Ireland will still find plenty of music sessions where the musicians are playing just for the love of it. It is hard to believe that fifty years ago there was no music in Irish pubs. In fact, the playing of music among groups of Irish people in pubs began overseas, principally among Irish emmigrant communities in the cities of Great Britain. London is widely regarded as the birthplace of the Irish music session. Flann O'Brien once wrote about bluebottles being the only sound in some out-of-the-way rural pubs in 1950s' Ireland. The Catholic Church, all powerful in the country after the state's foundation, did not take kindly to any type of enjoyment that they could not control, music and dancing included, and it was only with the opening up of Irish society in the 1960s that music became common in pubs in Ireland. Dublin had a number of famous 'singing pubs' from the 1930s onwards, but this was not a country-wide phenomenon. It was the latter part of the 1960s before a revival of folk music and ballad singing swept through the pubs of Dublin, bringing the likes of the Dubliners and singer Luke Kelly into public consciousness. While not all pubs have music, those that wish to attract the tourist crowds do, and sessions will generally be advertised in advance. However, the approach to timekeeping among musicians in Ireland can, at best, be described as 'loose'. In mitigation, if the circumstances are right and the drink is flowing, a good session can run long into the night. The instruments are usually acoustic, and may be any combination of accordions, fiddles, violins, guitars, mandolins and double bass, among others. The huge success of Riverdance in the 1990s unleashed a further wave of Irish traditional music across the world, and standards and provision have continued to rise. Building an Irish pub now in some far-flung corner of the world without providing some element of music would be as grievous a sin as having no Guinness. These days the visitor to Dublin is spoiled for choice when it comes to traditional music.

3. Fagan's

146 Lower Drumcondra Road, Dublin 9, 01 8375309,
www.faganspub.ie

First licensed in 1907, Fagan's is a pub very well-known to a large cross-section of Irish society. Indeed, some rural dwellers might only know this one pub in Dublin, given its proximity to Croke Park, the national headquarters of the Gaelic Athletic Association. For decades it has been a meeting point for people from all counties of Ireland before they move on to the hallowed stadium to see their teams compete in Gaelic football, hurling or camogie matches. After big matches this pub is a swirling sea of humanity with hundreds of people out in front meeting and greeting neighbours, friends and long-lost acquaintances. In this regard Fagan's can be considered a national institution. When Irish Taoiseach Bertie Ahern brought US President Bill Clinton here in 2001 it created a media stir. Bertie has long been partial to a pint of Bass in this, his favourite watering hole in his native Drumcondra. Originally Drumcondra Road was one of the four great roads of ancient Ireland, the Slighe Mhidhluachra, which entered the city from the north; it became a haunt of fashionable Victorians towards the end of the nineteenth century, a fact still reflected in some of the older housing stock, and in the austere façade of this highly regarded public house. Over time it mutated into an area of rented accommodation, with many of the old properties subdivided into flats and bedsits. Like other inner suburbs of Dublin, it has seen increasing gentrification in recent times, with houses converted back into family units, and an increasingly diverse range of restaurants, shops and cafes. Amidst the hustle and bustle, Fagan's has remained a constant.

This pub has seen many famous faces; a cursory glance at the pub's website shows portraits of characters as diverse as Hollywood actors Liam Neeson and Colin Farrell, footballers Roy Keane and Dennis Irwin, and musicians Bono and Boyzone. The list goes on and on. Inside there is a small front bar – very much a male-only establishment in the past – and a huge lounge out the back. Across the road there is a small park which doubles up as a beer garden when the crowds are about. For older people who remember Fagan's as a typical pub of the old school, the emphasis on food may come as a surprise, but such is the way things have moved in the pub trade. Many claim it to have some of the best food on this side of the city, with the Sunday roasts coming in for particular praise.

4. Gaffney's of Fairview

5 Fairview, Clontarf West, Dublin 3, 01 8339803,
www.facebook.com/GaffneyAndSon/

Gaffney's of Fairview claims to be the oldest pub on the north side of Dublin city, dating back to the early 1700s, when it was known as the Big Gun Inn. There are old written accounts of a sign here with a large cannon pointing across the road towards the sea, which came in as far as what is now the inner boundary of the reclaimed Fairview Park. At that time the pub was well known through its proximity to the Turnpike Gate, which collected tolls from those travelling to Clontarf and Howth. By 1834 the Big Gun Inn had mutated into two separate premises: Matthew Brown's at No. 4 and James Sweetman's at No. 5. In 1855 Thomas O'Mara bought both men out and ran a thriving business, helped in no small part by the corn chandlers and merchants who operated in the vicinity. O'Mara's tenure was to be short, and he was bought out by a Thomas Carroll in the early 1860s, who changed the name of the pub to the Emerald Isle Tavern. It was an era of nationalist-inspired pub names; the next door premises were called the Shamrock Inn.

It was only in 1921 that the pub got its current name, when it was purchased by Thomas Gaffney from Cavan. He and his son, Vincent,

built up the business significantly, and over time it assumed the roles of tea bonder, bottling yard, off licence and grocery. This fine establishment has been perfectly maintained over the years and is a fine example of the beautiful architectural detail evident in the great Victorian pubs of Dublin. It is well worth a visit. Gaffney's also has a literary connection as James Joyce lived nearby at No. 8 Royal Terrace for a short while and frequented the premises. The genteel atmosphere of this suburban pub is a world removed from the hustle and bustle of the Temple Bars of this world. It is a perfect place to while away some time in convivial company with great Guinness, if you so desire.

The Rounds System

The rounds system is not unique to Ireland, but it is central to drinking etiquette in the country. Originally an English invention, it was historically known as 'treating' and was once perceived as such a problem by temperance campaigners in Ireland that an 'anti-treating league' was established. In the rounds system, quite simply, each person in turn buys a drink for the other members of the group they are drinking with. It is frequently criticised as one of the factors underpinning the prevalence of binge-drinking in Ireland. In Australia and New Zealand, where the term 'shouting' is frequently used, it has also been a bone of contention for those concerned with alcohol abuse. Not 'getting a round in' is heavily frowned upon in Irish social life and, for better or worse, it is a part of pub etiquette that needs to be understood for a peaceful existence. The potential for misunderstanding is great when a person unfamiliar with the rounds system is brought to an Irish pub by a native. The Irish person will inevitably offer to buy a round of drinks for the assembled company but, crucially, this gesture of buying a round is not meant to be a gift, but rather a symbolic gesture established by historical precedent. By taking the initiative, the native demonstrates that he is the host, but it does not indicate he wants to be the only buyer. In trading rounds back and forth the other members of the group get to take turns acting in the roles of host and guest. Thus, the tradition of buying rounds builds camaraderie and makes each buyer a full member of the group. The embarrassment occurs when the newcomers do not appreciate the subtlety of the tradition. There is no doubt that round-buying can lead to drinking more than might be originally intended. During the First World War some pubs in Britain outlawed the buying of rounds to discourage intemperate ways in a time of national distress. Notwithstanding the occasional critic, the tradition still endures in Ireland, and for peace of mind it is generally in the best interests of the visitor to go with the flow.

5. The Gravediggers/Kavanagh's

1 Prospect Square, Glasnevin, Dublin 9, 01 8307978,
www.facebook.com/JohnKavanaghTheGravediggers

The Gravediggers pub in Glasnevin is a jewel in the crown of Dublin (and Irish) pubs. With its polished wood counters and stone floor it is also one of the darkest pubs anywhere and a true step back in time. There is even a ring board at the back, once a very popular game in pubs but long supplanted these days by darts and pool. Now under the stewardship of the eighth generation of the Kavanagh family, the pub claims to be the oldest establishment held by one family in the city.

The pub began trading when John O'Neill, owner of the Prince of Wales Hotel on the North Wall, converted part of his home into licensed premises in 1833, a year after the nearby Glasnevin Cemetery opened. At the time Irish patriot Daniel O'Connell was campaigning for a new road to be built to what were then the cemetery's main gates, so that funeral processions would not have to pass through a tollgate. As a result, funerals subsequently passed by the pub, proving a major boon for the business; the pub returned the favour by stocking Daniel O'Connell's Ale. John O'Neill was only the licensee for a year when he handed over the business as a wedding present to his daughter Suzanne and son-in-law John Kavanagh

in 1835. Such were the numbers of funeral attendees who went drinking after burial ceremonies in that era that Dublin Corporation saw fit to bring in a bylaw stipulating all interments had to be complete by noon.

John and Suzanne Kavanagh went on to have 25 children. Three of their sons served in the Union Army in the American Civil War; all were cited for bravery after the Battle of Gettysburg. In 1867 Joseph Kavanagh, one of the three military heroes, briefly returned to Ireland but was forced to return to America – where he spent another ten years – after being targeted by the British authorities as a Fenian activist. When he returned in 1877 he was no longer regarded as politically suspect and became the pub's new licensee. Shortly after he took over the business lost a significant amount of trade when the original cemetery gates were closed and a new entrance created on the Finglas Road. Joseph added a shooting range and a skittle alley to the premises, but they did not prove long-term successes. In 1907 the licence passed to Joseph's son, John H. Kavanagh, who died prematurely in 1920. The premises then passed to his wife, Josie. During her stewardship a grocery was added, which boosted business, and the bar became known as both 'Josie's' and 'The Widow's', nicknames that remained current until the 1950s. In 1973 Eugene Kavanagh left his job in Guinness and bought the pub from his family, running it up to the time of his untimely death in August 2015 at the age of 76. He told pub historian Cian Molloy that his father's 'lack of business enthusiasm meant that the pub wasn't gutted during the Formica and plastic era in the 1960s'.

Today, the pub is known widely as 'The Gravediggers', a nickname that, Eugene informed Molloy, was coined by workers at the newly built Glasnevin Industrial Estate in the 1970s:

> Lately, semi-yuppies have taken to calling it 'the Diggers'. I have never used either of these names to promote the pub. Indeed, I have never promoted the pub; my policy is to serve quality drink at a reasonable price and hope that word-of-mouth will bring more customers here. If the pub was used by gravediggers, there are not many of them about now. When the cemetery first opened, it had nine acres and sixty gravediggers; today it is seventy-nine acres and a dozen gravediggers with a JCB.

In 2014 the travel guide Lonely Planet published an ebook called *Secret Europe: 50 Truly Unforgettable Experiences to Inspire Your Next Trip to Europe*, in which Kavanagh's pub was only one of two places in Ireland mentioned; the other was the Cromane Peninsula in County Kerry. In a further claim to fame, the term 'are you going for a jar?' – widely used in Ireland to inquire if someone is going for a drink – is said to have originated in Kavanagh's.

Kavanagh's has featured on the silver screen a number of times. In 1970 the American film *Quackser Fortune Has a Cousin in the Bronx* was partially filmed in the bar. Starring Gene Wilder and Margot Kidder, and directed by Waris Hussein, it told the story of an unlikely romance between a manure seller and a rich American student. In one scene Wilder wheeled Kidder in his wheelbarrow from Saint Patrick's Cathedral to Glasnevin for a drink at Kavanagh's. The now deceased Wilder did not like the taste of Guinness and substituted it with Coca Cola with a Guinness head for the course of the shoot. The pub also featured in the Bob Hoskins film *The Woman Who Married Clark Gable*.

In the early 1980s Eugene Kavanagh added a lounge to the premises, the first on the north side of the city. However, it was not to become a venue for singing and music like most other similar establishments, as both are forbidden in the Gravediggers. Even the funeral of the legendary Luke Kelly of the Dubliners in 1984 did not see the universally enforced rule broken, as Ciarán Kavanagh told the BBC. A plethora of well-known musical stars, including the other members of the Dubliners, the Chieftains and U2, began to sing, but Eugene Kavanagh interrupted proceedings: 'My dad went out there and told everybody that they couldn't have any music or singing. "We don't allow it," he said. It would have been the best session ever, and especially in the pub that didn't have any music, it would have gone down in legend. But that was the rule – it's a place to just drink, it's always been about the drinking.'

When footage of a stag party singing in the toilets was circulated on social media in April 2016 it was possible to hear one of the participants saying 'he's going to have conniptions' – a Dublin slang word for a fit of anger. As expected, the barman went into the toilet and asked them to stop singing. Sportingly, he allowed them to finish the song, an atonal rendition of the Beatle's song 'I Will'.

The bar is now run by Anne, Ciarán, Anthony and Niall Kavanagh – all eighth-generation members of the family – along with their mother, Kathleen. Chef Ciarán oversaw the introduction of food to the lounge in the 2000s, and the pub has acquired a reputation for good fare, with particular plaudits for its tapas menu. Located in an unlikely place, a little off the beaten track, this is a Dublin pub not to be missed.

Publicans as Undertakers

The Coroners Act of 1864 decreed that, in the absence of a nearby hospital, a dead body could be brought to the nearest public house for storage until further arrangements were made. The beer cellars were cool and slowed down decomposition, and it became common for publicans to install a marble table in their cellars for autopsies. The *Freeman's Journal* of 9 April

1869 carried a story of a bus crash in Dublin. The injured were brought to Lawler's pub to be treated instead of the nearby Saint Mary's Asylum where nurses and doctors were in attendance. The editor complained that this was inappropriate, as the publican had no beds. Patrick Lawler saw fit to write to the paper to defend his actions:

> The body of Mrs. Byrne was brought into my house by the direction of Dr. Monks, and laid on the table of the taproom, where a large fire was burning. Blankets were at once brought down from the bed of my own family and wrapped round the body. Every possible effort was made to resuscitate her. My house was closed and business suspended while she remained there; everything required by the doctor and those in attendance were supplied by me.

This legislation was not removed from the statute books until 1962, and the dual role of publican and undertaker is still common in Ireland.

6. Harry Byrne's

107 Howth Road, Clontarf, Dublin 3, 01 8332650, www.harrybyrnes.ie

This beautiful pub traces its history back to 1798, when there was a coaching inn on this site licensed to a David Hallisey. Thankfully, the coach yard has survived as part of the modern-day car park. Images of the premises from that time depict a modest two-storey detached building with a thatched roof. The water supply for the inn was provided by a deep natural well, still a remarkable feature of the pub's interior. Inns at that time typically housed livery stables and a forge to deal with the needs of horses; they were rarely attended by locals, depending entirely on passing trade. At that time the passing road here was a notorious place for highway robbery. In 1809 the inn was designated a mail dispatch depot, further increasing its popularity. There are some gaps in the licensing history, but by 1861 the records show that a Thomas Carolan was running a pub and grocery on the site, as well as managing his farm. Carolan held an early licence, opening at 6 a.m. to provide refreshment to the many farmers and market gardeners who passed by on their way to the city markets. When the pub passed into the hands of James J. Corbett in 1906 he decided to demolish the existing building and started again from scratch. The result of his hard work is the now extant premises. Offaly man Harry Byrne came to work as an apprentice barman in 1920; 27 years later, after having worked for a while elsewhere, he returned to buy the pub for £22,000 – a huge sum of money at that time, and an indication of the successful business that existed. He remained at the helm until the early 1970s. The pub is divided into three areas: a main bar at the front, a small lounge area, and a big back bar. It boasts one of the best smoking areas of all Dublin pubs, with a widescreen television and comfortable seating. The affluent seaside suburb of Clontarf is only three kilometres by road, or one stop along the DART line, from the city centre, and is most celebrated as the location of the battle where Irish High King Brian Boru finally vanquished the Vikings in 1014. It was once a small fishing village, and later a haven for bathers from the city. These days it is a highly desirable residential area. This is a beautiful pub on this side of Dublin city.

7. The Hole in the Wall

345-347 Blackhorse Avenue, Phoenix Park, Dublin 7, 01 8389491,
www.holeinthewallpub.com

'One of the oldest public houses in Ireland, which for centuries has offered hospitality to all who cared to enter its doors'
Plaque at the entrance to the pub

This unassuming pub on the outskirts of the city has one of the longest bar counters in the country, and is the closest drinking establishment to the 1,700-acre Phoenix Park, the largest green space public amenity adjacent to a capital city in Europe. If the visitor to this area is here to see the nearby Phoenix Park Visitors' Centre it would be a shame not to call into this unique pub for a drink or

something to eat from the well-regarded menu. It is not a big pub, but makes up for what it lacks in size with a great atmosphere.

The Hole in the Wall claims to have once been a coach house dating back to 1651, and to have had a sign reading 'Ye Signe of Ye Blackhorse' outside, illustrated with a painting of a black horse. Such signs were once required by law due to widespread illiteracy. These premises were ideally located to fulfil its purpose as a coach house, as one of the main traffic arteries into the city passed by the front door. During the 1800s it mutated into a tavern and became a popular venue to drink and eat for those who came to listen to rabble-rousing speeches held in the nearby Phoenix Park. Daniel O'Connell – known as the 'Great Liberator' for achieving Catholic Emancipation for Ireland – was a particularly fiery orator who regularly drew massive crowds to his monster rallies – good news for the owners of the pub, who reciprocated by selling O'Connell's Ale, brewed by the politician's son.

Adding further to the customer base was the stationing of British soldiers in the nearby McKee Barracks in the Phoenix Park from 1891 to 1922. It was at this time the premises acquired its unique name from the practice of the then owner, Levinus Doyle, of delivering drink to thirsty members of the military, who had to remain outside the pub as they were not allowed to enter the premises by law, through a - yes you guessed it - hole in the wall. The establishment was only officially given the 'Hole in the Wall' designation in 1970 by owners P.J. and Mary McCaffrey, who have now been in charge for over forty years. Former President of Ireland Seán T. O' Kelly frequented the pub when he occupied nearby Áras an Uachtaráin - the Irish President's official residence - located in the Phoenix Park, and he is commemorated in the 'President's Snug'. This is a pub that holds a special place in the heart of its many fans.

8. The Hut/Mohan's

159 Phibsboro Road, Dublin 7, 01 8302238, www.thehutbar.ie

The Hut is one of the more unusually named pubs in Dublin and, once again, there are conflicting narratives as to the origin of the name. One story suggests that it got its title from the type of dwelling people lived in around this area more than 150 years ago, an indication of the poverty endemic in this part of the city at the time. Alternatively, the old dressing room at the nearby Dalymount Park, home of Bohemians soccer club, was known as 'the hut' because of its stone walls and galvanised roof, and the pub took the same name. Whichever story is true, there is no doubt that this is a beautiful pub in a part of Dublin city rarely visited by tourists. Phibsboro (or Phibsborough) is a funny place. It has the lowest rate of car ownership in the state, yet is constantly besieged by passing traffic with the ever-snarling Doyle's Corner at the centre of the scruffy mayhem. The lack of cycling lanes and the narrow footpaths make things that bit more difficult. The nearby pre-cast concrete-constructed 1960s' shopping centre, widely regarded as one of the ugliest buildings in the city, is not in line for any architectural awards but, thankfully, plans are afoot to replace it. Notwithstanding the tattered appearance and proliferation of charity shops, a closer look reveals many beautiful old Victorian and Edwardian buildings in the vicinity. In 2015 the area was designated an Architectural Conservation Area by

Dublin City Council to protect its 'architectural heritage and unique character'.

The Hut has a long association with sports followers. The 'Bohs' fans are always here in numbers when their team is playing at home. This historic pub is also close to Croke Park – the headquarters of the Gaelic Athletic Association, which runs Ireland's national games of hurling and football – another source of sporting fans on match days. Phibsboro is a hectic part of the city; the junction beside the pub is a constant swirl of activity, making the soothing interior a great place to get away from the hustle and bustle. Like other Victorian pubs it is principally characterised by dark wood, ornate detail, gas lamps and stained glass. The Hut is considered one of the most dog-friendly pubs in Dublin, another reason to make a detour to visit this wonderful piece of old Dublin. It is near to Glasnevin Cemetery and the National Botanic Gardens, and within walking distance of the city centre, so there really is little excuse.

Shebeens

Ireland gave the word 'shebeen' to the English language. A *síbín* (the Irish spelling, meaning illicit homemade whiskey) was a place where illegal alcohol was sold. These unlicensed premises were rudimentary, often cottages in the countryside or a simple room in an urban building. Anecdotal evidence suggests the survival of shebeens into the 1950s in Dublin tenement buildings and longer in remote areas of the countryside. Those in the tenements of Dublin proved notoriously difficult for the authorities to police because of warning systems put in place to let the owners and patrons know the law was in the area. It is also suggested by some authorities that members of the police force were reluctant to close shebeens down where in some cases there may have been financial arrangements in place to encourage the turning of a blind eye. With the demolitions of the inner-city tenements in the 1950s and 60s, the long-standing tradition of shebeens petered out.

The word 'shebeen' spread across the world and gained usage in Scotland, Canada, the United States, the English-speaking Caribbean, and parts of southern Africa, among others. 'Shebeen' is now used to describe drinking establishments in South African townships which are often legal. There are numerous pubs named 'Shebeen' or '*Síbín*' in Ireland, but they do not signify any particular type of establishment. However, despite the disappearance of illegal establishments, rumours still abound about shebeens in the more remote corners of Ireland.

9. L Mulligan Grocer

18 Stoneybatter, Dublin 7, 01 6709889, lmulligangrocer.com

This is the place to go if you are looking for a Mountain Man, a Crafty Hen, or a Belgian Blonde. Do not even think of trying to order a Guinness or a Budweiser here – it is craft beer all the way, and these are some of the labels. As the name suggests, L Mulligan Grocer in Stoneybatter once had a grocery shop in it; the rear section

of the pub is now a superb restaurant serving Irish produce with a clever creative twist. This is a pub that has led the way for others to follow, and is full of beautiful touches. From the menus which resemble school copy books, to the metal mathematical instrument boxes in which the bills are presented, the devil is truly in the detail. Tables, modelled on those typically found in old Irish kitchens, are reserved with letters spelled out in Scrabble trays, while jam jars wrapped in brown paper contain bouquets of freshly cut flowers. The pub is duly famous for its Scotch eggs, which come in meat and vegetarian guises. L Mulligan also provides accommodation in an apartment over the premises, where the lucky guest can avail of 'a few local beers in the fridge' on arrival. That has to be one of the best all-round packages in the city. The business is run by Seáneen Sullivan, Colin Hession and Michael Fogarty, who purchased the premises in 2010. It had previously been run by Larry Mulligan, who was both a publican and grocer.

10. Walsh's

6 Stoneybatter, Dublin 7, 01 6708647, www.walshsstoneybatter.ie

Cheesy Tuesdays are a popular affair in this old-world establishment at the heart of one of the trendiest areas of Dublin city. Each Tuesday night, a group of likeminded souls come together to sample cheeses that members have gathered from various sources. In the comfort of this warm and convivial pub they taste and discuss the produce, and there is usually enough for everyone in the premises to get a sample before the night is out. Those not in on the event may find it an unusual happening, but it has become a staple of the weekly schedule. If cheese is not your thing perhaps the regular and highly regarded table quizzes may take the visitor's fancy.

Walsh's is a straightforward pub with few gimmicks, but yet, in the modern way, it is not afraid to try new events to keep things fresh and interesting. While the hum of conversation pervades all corners of this fine establishment like a warm glow, and you could end up talking to all sorts who make up the eclectic clientele, it also has many nice cosy corners for those who prefer a quiet chat with

friends or a loved one. There is a beautiful and highly sought-after snug, complete with private serving hatch, if the visitor really wants to escape the hoi polloi. Stoneybatter has the sense of being a village, yet is only a stone's throw from the city centre, and Walsh's is the best pub in the village for many. Should the visitor be heading to the nearby L. Mulligan's for one of the best gastropub experiences in the city, Walsh's makes the perfect pre- or postprandial stopping-off point. The nearby Joinery Gallery brings an artistic crowd here when there is something on. The combination of old-school regulars and young urbanites make this is a great example of a true twenty-first-century Dublin pub. It is the type of establishment that will ensure the continued greatness of the pub-going tradition in Ireland's capital city.

Dublin South County

1. The Blue Light

Barnacullia, Sandyford, County Dublin, 01 2160487, thebluelight.ie

The Blue Light is a special pub, commanding a spectacular view over the city of Dublin, located over 700 feet above sea level. Established in 1870 and located in Barnacullia –translated from the Irish as 'top of the woods' – in the foothills of the Dublin Mountains, it may be the most difficult of all pubs to get to on this list, but is well worth the trip on a fine day, as the many customers who travel up here at the merest hint of good weather can attest.

The name of the pub is said to have originated in the mid-1800s. When the custom officers in Dún Laoghaire Harbour finished work a light signal would be sent up the hill to this location. Another light signal would then be sent back out into the bay, using a blue ship's lantern, to let smugglers know that the coast was clear to land illegal goods such as alcohol and tobacco. Barnacullia also has a venerable, and more legal, tradition of quarrying granite; the local

stone has been used to build some of Dublin's finest buildings and churches. The Blue Light is a great example of a rural Irish pub, with peat fires and good music, in close proximity to a large urban area. Once ensconced here the visitor is totally oblivious to the teeming hordes of the nearby metropolis. The pub has three areas: a lounge, a smaller bar and an impressive outdoor courtyard. The bar and the lounge are divided into upper and lower levels. World-famous rock band U2 used to gig here in the late 1970s, and have enjoyed pints here regularly over the decades. It is rumoured Bono once wanted to buy the pub, but the owner was not interested in selling. There is a second U2 story attached to the Blue Light. In 1989 bass guitarist Adam Clayton was arrested for possession of drugs in the car park here. During a routine check by Gardaí they found nineteen grams of cannabis in his possession. He was charged with suspicion of dealing, fined, and released with a warning.

For those who would like an extended stay at this outstanding pub the owners have an upstairs apartment known as the 'Blue Light Loft' which can be rented for a minimum of two nights at a time. It is almost too good to be true.

2. Finnegan's

1 Sorrento Road, Dalkey, County Dublin, 01 2858505,
www.finnegans.ie

When the security detail were choosing an appropriate place to bring American First Lady Michelle Obama and her children, Malia and Sasha, on their visit to Ireland in 2013 they chose this hostelry, frequented by many of the great and the good of Irish society who live in this affluent seaside suburb. If it is good enough for rock singer Bono and other members of supergroup U2 then it had to be an appropriate place to bring the wife and children of Barack Obama. Finnegan's is one of the sixteen remaining Victorian-era pubs in Dublin and, despite being a hike from the city centre, it is well worth a trip, particularly on a fine day. Besides, it is on the DART (Dublin Area Rapid Transport) light railway line, which, some guide books contend, commands some of the finest views from any railway line in Europe.

Dalkey was chosen by the Danish Vikings as a place of habitation because of its natural port, and it has continued to be a desirable location to reside ever since. George Bernard Shaw was the first celebrated writer to take up residency in the area, and he has been followed ever since by luminaries from a plethora of different fields.

The Finnegan family have a well-established reputation as publicans. The pub is run by Dan Finnegan and his sons, while his brothers Ned, James and Hugh have also run successful pubs in Dublin and Wicklow. Although there were major refurbishments in 2001 and 2005, the pub has retained the Victorian sensibility dating back to its foundation in 1862. In 1989 Finnegan's commenced selling food under the watchful eye of the now sadly deceased Paul Finnegan, and soon its Sorrento Lounge established a stellar reputation. When Michelle Obama ate here it was covered on live television by CBS Los Angeles' *Breakfast Show* from a neighbouring garden. The restaurant has fed a who's who of global stars, including Tom Cruise, Mel Gibson, Brad Pitt and Salman Rushdie. Finnegan's pub is the perfect place to eat and drink after a bracing walk on the nearby beach and is well worth a trip out from the city.

A Fourteen-Year-Long Pub Strike

Downey's pub in Dún Laoghaire once had a strike by staff that lasted fourteen years. It started when a unionised barman was sacked in March 1939. After the rest of the staff went on strike, in support of their colleague, they too were let go. For the next fourteen years they picketed the pub in daily shifts and made international headlines. When an Irish fishing boat encountered a German U-boat during the Second World War, the chief officer of the submarine reputedly asked 'if the strike was still on in Downey's'. The pub no longer exists and has been replaced by the Dún Laoghaire shopping centre and cinema.

3. Johnnie Fox's

*Ballybetadh Road, Glencullen, County Dublin, 01 2955647,
www.johnniefoxs.com*

Johnnie Fox's has been at the centre of Glencullen village since 1798, the year Theobald Wolfe Tone led an infamous failed uprising against the British colonial powers. The site the pub now occupies was originally a small farm, a fact reflected in the names of sections of the pub. The dining area is called 'The Pig House' and the small courtyard is called 'The Haggart', a term used to denote a small closed-off area on an Irish farm.

Johnnie Fox's, about 35 minutes from Dublin city centre by car, boasts of being the highest pub in Dublin, and has a truly amazing view of the city below. It may also be the only pub in the country with a grave built into the wall.

The village of Glencullen has several connections of historical interest, making for a further good excuse to travel out this way. The Colonel's House in the village was once used as a hideaway by Michael Collins during the War of Independence, while Daniel O'Connell was a frequent patron of the pub in earlier times. Fox's, like many other pubs in Dublin, claims to have been a meeting place for leaders during the 1916 Rising. Glencullen has a Bronze Age wedge tomb on the south-eastern slopes of Two Rock Mountain at Ballyedmonduff known as the 'Giant's Grave', as well as a significant standing stone and an earthen burial mound at Newtown Hill to occupy the visitor.

Johnnie Fox's has a long-standing connection with traditional Irish music. In the early 1950s nights of music and storytelling were recorded here and later broadcast on RTE Radio 1, the main station of the national broadcaster.

The list of famous visitors listed on the pub's website must be the longest in the country. Politicians who have set foot here include former Prime Minister of Australia John Howard, Prince Phillippe of Spain, President Vaclav Havel of the Czech Republic, Prince Joachim of Denmark, and former leader of the British Labour Party Neil Kinnock. Those from the big screen who have imbibed here include

Brad Pitt, Meryl Streep, Pierce Brosnan and Ben Kingley, while luminaries of the music industry including the Rolling Stones, Robbie
Williams, Bryan Adams and Celine Dion have paused here for a
libation. Some famous singers, musicians and bands, not normally
associated with the intimacy of a public house, have even taken a turn
performing here, including the Pogues, Boyzone and the Hot House
Flowers. The list of famous sportspeople who crossed the threshold
is barely believable and includes such icons as boxer Mohammed
Ali, the Chicago Bears football team, the Polish soccer team, tennis
player Boris Becker, renowned mountaineer Chris Bonnington, and
a host of star soccer players. Notable literary visitors have included
Salman Rushdie, and old Irish reliables Patrick Kavanagh and
Brendan Behan. The list goes on and on.

In an interview with the *Irish Independent*, owner Tony McMahon
stressed the difference between Fox's and the vast majority of other
pubs in the country. Despite the fact that there are only 400 people
living within a two-and-a-half-mile radius the restaurant is always
booked out and the bar is always busy. It is a 'destination pub', the
mythical beast desired by rural publicans all over the country of
Ireland but only granted to a lucky few.

In recent years the pub has become famous for its 'Hooley Night'
– a combined evening of dinner and traditional Irish music, dancing
and storytelling. Johnnie Fox's has everything possible the tourist
could need in an Irish pub, if they are happy to put up with the
throngs of visitors. It is a unique place.

Dublin North County

1. Gibney's

6 New Street, Malahide, County Dublin, 01 8450606,
www.gibneys.com

This historic pub in the beautiful village of Malahide, nine miles by coastal road from O'Connell Street, is well worth a trip away from the city centre. It was acquired by the Gibney family in 1937 for £2,500, having previously traded as the Abercorn Tavern under the stewardship of Henry Barton Cooke since 1890. James Joseph Gibney, the first of the family to put his name above the door, was from a family steeped in the pub trade, as they also owned the Royal Hotel in Howth, the Phoenix Bar in Parkgate Street (yet another former haunt of Michael Collins) and the Abbey Tavern in Howth. When James Joseph took charge this hostelry had a strong rural flavour and, probably more noticeably, a strong rural smell, as it contained an apple orchard and piggery.

The Well Room is a highlight of this beautifully preserved and hugely popular venue. Holding 14,000 gallons of water, it once functioned as the village well in addition to its use by the publicans for washing bottles before they were filled as part of the establishment's bottling enterprise. The water, like that in so many old wells, is said to have curative powers, so between the good Guinness and magic elixir of the aqua vitae there is ample reason to make a trip here for a restorative interlude.

For those of a historic bent there is evidence of a previous pub on this site: the Golden Lion Inn dated back to the 1740s, a time when Malahide was famous for green-finned oysters and cotton and silk manufacturing, as well as being home to a substantial salt works and coal yard. The historic village was also once famous for the circuses held on the village green – it became known locally as 'theatreland' – and revellers frequented the famed drinking establishment. The Golden Lion ceased to operate in the early part of the nineteenth century, but there is evidence of a public house on the site after the arrival of the Malahide railway in 1845.

Modern-day Gibney's might look small from the outside, but it is an extensive premises with a bar, two lounges, the aforementioned Well Room and an impressive courtyard, as well as the curiously named Caughoo Bar. The latter gained its name from a famous horse of the same name who won a mist-and-fog-bound British Grand National at Aintree in the United Kingdom in 1947. If the visitor is in this beautiful part of Dublin it would be a shame not to drop in.

2. The Harbour Bar (formerly the Cock Tavern)

18 Church Street, Howth, Dublin 13, 01 3004333,
www.facebook.com/HarbourBarHowth

Howth was once just a tiny fishing village. Now this beautiful peninsula is a thriving suburb of Dublin, but it still manages to retain its unique homely feel. The name Howth is thought to be of Norse origin, perhaps being derived from the Old Norse *Hǫfuð* ('head' in English). Norse Vikings first invaded Howth in 819 and were a local powerbase until usurped by the Anglo-Normans in 1177. A day trip from the city on the DART would pay rich dividends for the visitor with an interest in beautiful scenery and intriguing history. The highlight of the trip, apart from the pubs, might be Howth Castle, which is both one of the oldest occupied buildings in Ireland and a frequent sight on the silver screen. The village played an important role in the struggle for Irish freedom, because it was here Erskine Childers landed illegal guns for the Irish Volunteers which were used in the 1916 Rising. Howth has long been a place for the great and the good to live, and former and current residents include poet William Butler Yeats, broadcaster Gay Byrne, and actor Brendan Gleeson.

While this pub changed name from the Cock Tavern to the Harbour Bar in 2016, records show that the latter name had previously been used for licensed premises on this site. Many may still refer to it as the Cock Tavern as the new owners have opted to keep the painting of the cock on the outside of the building.

There is no doubting the changes inside the bar. Previous signs of disco motifs have been supplanted by dark woods, open fires and exposed brick, while the swing-door two-seat snug is a thing of beauty. At the back the bar has opened the first craft beer house on the peninsula of Howth, complete with its own micro-brewery. For those interested in the mechanics of the brewing process, there are three 1,000-litre kettles on display behind glass which feed directly into the taps. This is the brave new world of the artisan craft brew pub, although this is not one where they have thrown the baby out with the bath water: Guinness is still to be had on tap. The Harbour Bar has a particularly good reputation for live music, and visitors are deeply enamoured of the big open fire, not something to be had everywhere. This is a real pub with a really good atmosphere in a lovely part of Dublin.

Irish Civil War

The tragedy of the Irish Civil War has continued to resonate through the decades. In a deeply divisive conflict, neighbour sometimes fought neighbour and families were ripped asunder. The strife arose over differences concerning the Anglo-Irish Treaty, the agreement ratified between Britain and Ireland at the end of the War of Independence. Republicans saw the terms of the treaty as a betrayal of what they had first fought for in the Easter Rising of 1916. Nationalists – often called Free Staters – agreed with the terms of the Treaty, albeit recognising it was imperfect. In the words of Michael Collins they saw it as providing not freedom but the 'freedom to achieve freedom'. In June 1922 a bitter and gruesome guerrilla campaign began between the opposing factions. Eleven months of sporadic and often brutal incidents resulted in the Anti-Treaty/Republican forces realising that their dwindling resources would never bring success and they laid down their weapons. The consequences of the Civil War were far-reaching. The two main political parties in the Republic of Ireland – Fianna Fáil and Fine Gael – have their roots in the Anti-Treaty and Free State supporters respectively. While the Civil War does not directly impinge on modern Irish life it still engenders strong emotions in many people.

3. The Man O'War Bar and Restaurant

Courtlough, Balbriggan, County Dublin, 01 8415528,
www.manowar.ie

The intriguingly named Man O'War, in the hills of north county Dublin, is a small geographical area centred on the townlands of Courtlough, Malhenry and Palmerstown, about 24 kilometres north of the city centre, located between the towns of Skerries, Lusk and Balbriggan. This pub is a real find, in the least likely of places. Almost inevitably, there are conflicting stories as to the origins of the place name. Perhaps the most intriguing one is that of the 'Turk's Head'. For many years, the tale goes, a wooden carving depicting a Turk's head adorned a pillar outside the pub. It was said that this unusual figurine, depicting the Greek god Hercules, came from a shipwrecked man o'war ship and gave the area its name. Alternatively, this area was once covered by trees which were felled and used to construct British man o'war ships. A further theory suggests the name may have come from the Irish word 'bharr' meaning 'middle height', a reference to this area being located halfway up the north Dublin hills.

From the outside, the Man O'War pub looks like nothing more than a quaint country cottage. Inside it is a sight to behold: beautiful open fires, a cornucopia of knickknacks and – wonder of wonders – a live tree growing up through the centre of the room and out through the roof. The pub claims to have been here since 1595, which would, if true, make it one of the oldest in the country. The passing road was once the main route between Dublin and Belfast, and in 1732 an Act of Parliament established the Dublin to Dunleer turnpike as a tolled road, with a booth situated at this junction. It existed until 1855. The pub was perfectly located halfway along the route, and numbers Irish freedom fighter Theobald Wolfe Tone among its former visitors; apparently he stopped here for his breakfast in 1792. Well-known travel writer Dr John Gamble stopped over and wrote about it. The road was frequented by some unsavoury characters back in the day, none more notorious than Collier the Highway Man.

The pub is unreservedly aimed firmly at the food market, which is not surprising given its location in the countryside and the ever-tighter restrictions on drink-driving and the general move away from drink-only socialising patterns. Those who are looking for entertainment will not be disappointed. Traditional Irish group the Curragh and professional Irish dancing troupes are regulars here, while in July bikers from all over gather for the famous Skerries meet. In May 2016 the pub organised a hugely successful music festival. This establishment is constantly striving to update the product to keep it fresh without disregarding the core virtues of what makes places like it so good: hospitality, conviviality and good service.

4. Stoop Your Head

Harbour Road, Skerries, County Dublin, 01 8492085,
www.stoopyourhead.ie

This quaintly named establishment has established a formidable reputation for great pub food in north Dublin. Its proximity to the nearby fishing fleet in Skerries mean its signature half-and-half seafood dish– half Dublin Bay prawns and half Rockabill crab claws - is as fresh as any in the country. This is a gastropub with the emphasis solidly on gastro, and customers travel from all over to sample the seafood delights on offer in this picturesque establishment. It might not be everyone's idea of an Irish pub, but what they do here they do exceptionally well. Combined with the wonderful views over the harbour, this pub is a must for those who want to combine the culinary with the grain and grape. That said, there is nothing stopping anyone just dropping in for a drink and sitting at the bar, but in ventures like Stoop Your Head this is an increasing rarity. As drinking habits changed in Ireland over recent decades the only option for many pubs who wished to remain viable was to go down the food route. Publicans routinely note that whereas food sales may have been 20 per cent of their sales a decade ago this has now turned 180 degrees, with food accounting for 80 per cent of their turnover and alcohol making up the 20-per-cent-segment. This establishment is a trailblazer in this regard. Stoop Your Head does not take bookings, so be prepared to wait.

When under the ownership of Michael Duffy the pub was officially known as Grosvenor House. His constant exhortations to customers to mind their head as they moved from one section of the pub to another, passing under a low beam, led to the pub becoming known as Stoop Your Head. The name stuck. Old Stoop, as Duffy was known, ran a male-only establishment which, he liked to think, was a 'respectable house', but, by all accounts, contained minimal design fripperies. All has now changed, and this pub is now a house of gastronomic delights.

West Dublin

1. Strawberry Hall

Strawberry Beds, Chapelizod, Dublin 20, 01 8213002,
www.facebook.com/thestrawberryhall

The Strawberry Beds was once a favourite place for honeymooners to whisper sweet nothings before foreign travel came into vogue; it was also the recreational choice of James Joyce, where, during his spare time, he came to loll on the river bank contemplating his next masterpiece. This beautiful woodland area of the Liffey Valley provides a delightful backdrop to this old-world establishment. In recent years this slightly out-of-the-way pub has gained a reputation for putting on one of the best Christmas lights display of any pub in Dublin. It is also probably the only remaining pub in Dublin, if not Ireland, with a bagatelle table. The seventeenth-century billiards game was once a popular pastime in hostelries but has long since fallen out of favour; the only Bagatelle known in Dublin these days is a band who have had considerable success singing about the Irish capital, most notably with the song 'Summer in Dublin'.

The Strawberry Hall claims to be Dublin's second oldest pub – but all claims of pub ages come with a compulsory health warning as it is an area fraught with logistical and legal difficulty – and is located roughly halfway between the villages of Chapelizod and Lucan. It takes a little effort to get here, as the nearest bus stop is nearly three kilometres away, but the intrepid visitor will not be disappointed. It should not take much effort to work out that this unique area got its name from the once-upon-a-time production of strawberries. At that time producers sold strawberries, held in lettuce leaves, from tables on the side of the road to those who passed this way. Looking in over the walls along the road here it is possible to see the remains of terracing used to grow the fruit. The only drawback to this special place is the impunity with which motorists use the road as a shortcut. However, it is well-nigh impossible to find anyone who knows this pub with anything negative to say; it is consistently pointed to as a haven from the hustle and bustle of the city, and a perfect antidote to the frenetic world of Christmas shopping, while still keeping the spirit of the occasion alive. The pub claims to have the best pint of Guinness in West Dublin and it would be churlish to disagree. The Strawberry Hall is also a popular venue for music lovers, with a fine reputation for blues and traditional Irish, and if you happen to be here on a Monday night you will have the pleasure of hearing the excellent house band Last Straw. What makes this pub stand out, literally and metaphorically, is the fact that it is out on its own in the countryside, despite being so close to the city centre. The owners have also instituted an admirable free bus service for their patrons to and from the surrounding areas of Castleknock, Carpenterstown, Coolmine, Clonsilla, Lucan, Blanchardstown, Cabra, Chapelizod and Ashtown. There has been a lot of lip service and handwringing about the effect of drink-driving legislation on pub attendance in Ireland, particularly those located in the rural hinterland. Here is a fine example of a business which has done something about it.

Those who frequent this venerable establishment talk about its addictive nature. The beer garden comes in for particular high praise as a pleasant place to while away a few hours on a good summer's day. What more could you want?

Pub Numbers

Ireland is home to over 7,000 pubs, according to a 2017 report published by the Drinks Industry Group of Ireland (DIGI) and authored by Dublin City University (DCU) economist Anthony Foley. According to Foley and his associates Ireland has 7,193 pubs, as well as 3,161 off-licences, 2,406 restaurants and 983 hotels. Of the pubs, 773 were registered in Dublin city and county, down 1.7 per cent compared with the 786 recorded in 2005, but up from a low of 741 in 2012. For political buffs the number of pubs in each of the designated political constituencies, as calculated by the DIGI report, may be of interest:

- Dublin Bay North: 89
- Dublin Bay South: 70
- Dublin Central: 54
- Dublin Fingal: 86
- Dublin Mid-West: 66
- Dublin North-West: 55
- Dublin Rathdown: 53
- Dublin South-Central: 70
- Dublin South-West: 88
- Dublin West: 69
- Dún Laoghaire: 72

AIB's 2018 *Outlook: Pubs* report counted 772 pubs in Dublin, one for every 1,649 people in the capital. (The comparable figure for Cork was 543. The county with the fewest people per pub is Mayo, with 323 people for every pub in the county. Other counties with low numbers of people per pub include Kerry (one pub for every 334 people), Tipperary (one pub per 350 people) and Clare (one pub for every 383 people).)

Index

B

Bailey, The 12
Bank Bar and Restaurant, The 16
Bar With No Name, The 18
Barber's, The 162
Bernard Shaw, The 19
Bleeding Horse, The 21
Blue Light, The 183
Bowe's 24
Brazen Head, The 28
Bruxelles 31

C

Cafe en Seine 34
Capstan Bar, The (John Fallon's) 71
Cassidy's 36
Castle Lounge/Grogan's 59
Church, The 128
Cobblestone, The 164
Confession Box, The 131

D

Davy Byrne's 38
Devitt's 43
Doheny and Nesbitt 45

Dropping Well, The 152
Duke, The 49

F

Fagan's 166
Farrier and Draper 52
Ferryman, The 53
Finnegan's 184

G

Gaffney's of Fairview 168
George, The 56
Gibney's 188
Gravediggers, The/Kavanagh's 170
Gravity Bar, The, at the Guinness Storehouse 58
Grogan's/Castle Lounge 59

H

Hacienda, The 135
Harbour Bar, The (formerly the Cock Tavern) 189
Harry Byrne's 174
Hartigan's 63

Hole in the Wall, The   175
Horseshoe Bar, The, in the Shel-
    bourne Hotel   64
Hut, The/Mohan's   177

I

International Bar, The   67

J

Jack Nealon's   137
Jimmy Rabbitte's   70
John Fallon's (The Capstan Bar)   71
Johnnie Fox's   186

K

Kavanagh's/The Gravediggers   170
Kehoe's   74

L

L Mulligan Grocer   179
Library Bar, The, at the Central
    Hotel   78
Long Hall, The   79
Lord Edward, The   82

M

Madigan's   139
Man O'War Bar and Restaurant,
    The   191
Mary's Bar   84
McDaid's   87
Mohan's/The Hut   177
Mulligan's   90

N

Neary's   93
Norseman, The   95

O

Oarsman, The   154
O'Connell's Bar   97
O'Donoghue's   98
Old Spot, The   155
Old Stand, The   100
O'Neill's   103
Oval, The   141

P

Palace Bar, The   105
Pantibar   143
Peruke and Periwig   108
Piper's Corner, The   145
P. Mac's   109
Porterhouse Central, The   110
Porterhouse, The, Temple Bar
    112

R

Royal Oak, Kilmainham   156
Ruin Bar   113
Ryan's of Parkgate Street   147

S

Searson's   113
Slattery's of Capel Street   150
Slattery's of Rathmines   157
Stag's Head, The   115
Stoop Your Head   192

Strawberry Hall   194
Swan, The   117

W

Walsh's   181
Whelan's   126

T

Toner's   121

Y

Yellow House, The   160

V

Vintage Cocktail Club, The   123